How Water Can Help You Change Your Life

David Broward

CONTENTS

PREFACE

If we read the ancient spiritual texts word by word, focusing in particular on the word "water", we discover some very peculiar, intriguing things. First, it seems that water existed long before our known Universe, including our Earth, came into existence.

For example, let's make a quick review of the story of Creation of the Heaven and the Earth, depicted in the Book of Genesis. Although I'm pretty sure that most of you are familiar with the story, let's make however a throughout analysis of the first ten verses, paying attention in particular to the word "water".

In the first verse of the Bible we read that *"In the beginning God created the heaven and the earth."* (Genesis 1:1, KJV).

And the book continues by narrating how our visible Universe came into existence. However, before the Creation process to begin, before God made the stars, the earth, the plants and the animals, we read that *"the earth was without form, and void; and darkness was upon the face of the deep.* **And the Spirit of God moved upon the face of the waters.**" (Genesis 1:2, emphasis added)

In the first day, *"God divided the light from the darkness. And God called the light Day, and the darkness he called Night."* (Genesis 1:3-5).

During the second day of Creation, we notice another very interesting statement regarding water: *"God said,* **Let there be a firmament in the midst of the waters, and let it divide the waters from the waters."** (Genesis 1:6, emphasis added)

So, God *"made the firmament, and* **divided the waters which were under the firmament from the waters which were above the firmament"** (Genesis 1:7), and *"God called the firmament Heaven. And the evening and the morning were the second day."* (Genesis 1:8).

Continuing with the story, we read how God created the *"lights in the firmament of the heaven"*, *"the stars"*, and *"two great lights; the greater light to rule the day, and the lesser light to rule the night"* (the fourth day, Genesis 1:15-19), while in the sixth day, *"God said, Let us make man in our image, after our likeness"* (Genesis 1:26)

However, if we pay attention to the text, in the morning of the third day, *"God said,* **Let the waters under the heaven be gathered together unto one place, and let the dry land appear:** *and it was so. And God called the dry land Earth; and the gathering together of the waters called he Seas…"* (Genesis 1:9-10, emphasis added).

Thus, according to the Bible, the Earth was created <u>ONLY AFTER</u> God divided *"the waters from the waters"* (Genesis 1:6), and <u>AFTER</u> He gathered together *"the waters under the heaven."* (Genesis 1:9)

Even more, the *"Spirit of God moved upon the face of the waters"* (Genesis 1:2) long before He said *"Let the waters bring forth abundantly the moving creature that hath life, and fowl that may fly above the earth in the open firmament of heaven"* (Genesis 1:20), and before He made *"male and female"* (Genesis 1:27), *"in our image, after our likeness"* (Genesis 1:26).

This particular depiction of the process of Creation is encountered in every single version of the Bible, regardless of its various and numerous translations. In all the versions, in the first verses we read that **"The Spirit of God"** (sometimes translated as *"the Wind"*, *"the Breath"*, *"the Mind"* or *"Ruach Elohim"*) **"moved"** (or, depending on the translation, was *"moving"*, *"hovering"*, *"fluttering"* or *"brooding"*) **"upon"** (or *"over"*) *"the face of the* **waters"** (or, in some translations, *"the surface of the water(s)"*).

Interestingly, this tale, found in one of mankind's oldest books, shockingly resembles our current scientific approach regarding the formation of the Universe.

To understand what I mean, allow me to make an overall description of the mainstream "Big Bang" theory. Cosmologists and astrophysicists propose that our Universe emerged from a singularity, some 13.8 billion years ago.

Before the singularity started to expand, (as yet scientists are not sure where this singularity came from or how it appeared), there was no time, space or matter. All the forces known today as ruling the Universe (the nuclear forces, electromagnetism and gravity) were united into a single force. In Bible's words, *"darkness was upon the face of the deep. And the Spirit of God moved upon the face of the waters."*

The singularity started to expand, and during the first 240,000 – 300,000 years after the "Big Bang" (the period known as the Era of Recombination), the matter and the antimatter annihilated each other and created light. This primordial light is detectable today in the form of cosmic microwave background radiation. In a much simpler depiction, the Bible narrates that in the first day *"God said, Let there be light"* (Genesis 1:3), He *"divided the light from the darkness"* (Genesis 1:4), and *"God called the light Day, and the darkness he called Night. And the evening and the morning were the first day."* (Genesis 1:5)

According to cosmologists, the primordial nucleosynthesis took place long before the light to appear (in about the first 10 seconds to 20 minutes after the Big Bang), and the first chemical element was deuterium, a hydrogen isotope (also known as heavy hydrogen, ^2H or D).

Now, if we look at the etymology of the word "hydrogen", we see that the word comes from the Greek *hudrō/ hydro*, (meaning *"water"*) and *-genēs/ - gen* (meaning giving *"rise to"* or *"producing"*), thus, hydrogen basically means *"water-former"*.

There are a few interesting things about this *"water-former"*. It is known for its non-toxic, non-metallic and highly combustible properties and is considered the lightest, smallest and simplest chemical element. It also the most abundant element in the Universe, accounting for about 75% of its normal matter by mass and more than 90% of all the atoms.

According to classic Physics, without the existence of the strong nuclear force (which is more than 100 times stronger than the electromagnetic force), there would be no nuclei, except for individual protons and neutrons. The neutrons would decay radioactively and disappear in a short time, while the protons would become the nuclei of hydrogen atoms. So basically, pretty much everything in the Universe would be composed of *"water-former"* (or hydrogen).

Today, we consider common knowledge that two parts of hydrogen and one part of oxygen form the substance we refer to as "water". But here's another very intriguing fact about water: at standard ambient temperature and pressure (used in Chemistry as the reference with the temperature of 25 °C and a pressure of 1 atm), we can clearly see the water's liquid form, and we use it in countless ways, from our daily hydration to cooking, and from taking a shower to flush the toilet. This, despite the fact that under the same conditions, its components, both hydrogen and oxygen, are tasteless, odourless and colourless (thus, invisible to our physical senses).

For the sake of comparison, for oxygen or hydrogen to exist in liquid form (at standard atmospheric pressure), they have to be cooled down to temperatures way below zero Celsius (-218.79 °C for oxygen and -252.87 °C for hydrogen respectively).

In fact, water is THE ONLY substance found in Nature that exists in three visible states – liquid, solid (as ice) and gaseous (as steam) –, albeit is made of two invisible, gaseous substances.

As far as regarding the water, the story found in the Bible not only that matches our modern astronomic and cosmologic views, but it is also in agreement with the concepts found in Archaeology, Geography, Palaeontology, Anthropology, Geology, Abiogenesis and many other fields of science. It even agrees with the famous theory of Evolution, proposed by Charles Darwin not even 200 years ago.

If we look at the big picture, as a condition for the plants and animals to appear, it has to be in the first place the Earth, as a physical support where life to occur. It makes perfect sense, and both, science and religion, agree with this fact. Both also agree that we need water in order to survive, and there's life as we know wherever there is water on this Blue Planet.

Still, straight from water's perspective, the Christian's Holy Book has a different approach regarding water. According to the Bible, before the matter and the antimatter annihilated each other (or God separated *"the Light from the*

Darkness"), and before the four main forces known today as ruling the Universe separated from the initial, primordial force, *"the Spirit of God moved upon the face of the waters"*.

We'll see in the following pages if the rest of the claims found in the Bible – that God made a *"firmament in the midst of the waters"*, *"divided the waters which were under the firmament from the waters which were above the firmament"* and gathered together the *"waters under the heaven"* – are confirmed by our current scientific understanding.

This intriguing idea that water existed before anything else came into existence is encountered in all the Abrahamic religions. Billions of Christians, Muslims and Jews alike, from all over the world, are sharing the same story regarding the Origin of the Creation.

In the Hebrew Book of Bereshit of the Written Torah we find (pretty much) the same narration, while in the Qur'an we read that it is He *"who has created the heavens and the earth in six aeons;* **and [ever since He has willed to create life,] the throne of His almightiness has rested upon water"** (The Qur'an, *Hud* 11:7). The Qur'an also narrates that it is *"God who has **created all animals out of water"** (The Qur'an, *An-Nur* 24.45), and **"out of this [very] water has created man"** (The Qur'an, *Al-Furqan* 25.54, emphasis added).

What I found particularly fascinating about this concept is that it is encountered in ALL THE ANCIENT SPIRITUAL BELIEFS, no matter how far we'd look back into our known history.

From Native Americans and African communities – who were strongly influenced by their profound connection with Nature, and although their myths were not written down until recently, existed for thousands of years in spoken form –, to ancient Egyptians and Babylonians (for whom we have archaeological and historical evidences), all our forefathers regarded water as the *"Origin of Everything"*.

For example, one of the Cherokee Creation myths narrates that **"in the beginning, there was just water.** *All the animals lived above it and the sky was overcrowded. They were all curious about what was beneath the water and one day Dayuni'si, the water beetle, volunteered to explore it. He explored the surface but could not find any solid ground. He explored below the surface to the bottom and all he found was mud which he brought back to the surface. After collecting the mud, it began to grow in size and spread outwards until it became the Earth as we know it."* (emphasis added)

In the Mayan K'iche' *Popol Vuh* (meaning 'Book of the People'), we read that in the beginning, *"all was in suspense, all calm, in silence; all motionless, still, and the expanse of the sky was empty... There was neither man, nor animal, birds, fishes, crabs, trees, stones, caves, ravines, grasses, nor forests; there was only the sky. The surface of the earth had not appeared.* **There was only the calm sea and the great expanse of the sky. There was nothing brought together, nothing which could** *make a noise, nor anything which might move, or tremble, or could make noise in the sky. There was nothing standing; only the calm water, the placid sea, alone and tranquil. Nothing existed. There was only immobility and silence in the darkness, in the night. Only the Creator, the Maker, Tepeu, Gucumatz, the Forefathers, were in the water surrounded with light."* (emphasis added)

According to the ancient Egyptian Creation Myth, the *zep tepi* (the "first event") took place in *Nu* (*Nun* or *Naunet*, depending on the translation), the dark, endless, lifeless, everlasting and limitless water.

In the Hindu *Knowledge of the Verses* (the *Rig Veda*), which is one of the oldest Hindu religious text (and probably the world's oldest spiritual text in continued use), we read that in the beginning…

"There was neither aught nor naught, nor air, nor sky beyond.
What covered all? Where rested all? In watery gulf profound?
Nor death was then, nor deathlessness, nor change of night and day.
The One breathed calmly, self-sustained; nought else beyond it lay.
Gloom, hid in gloom, existed first - one sea, eluding view."

In the Babylonian *Enûma Eliš* (also known as the *Seven Tablets of Creation*) all the Gods, and subsequently all beings, arose from the fusion of *Apsu* (the fresh water) and *Tiamat,* the salt water. In the Greek mythology, *Chaos* (the large void encompassing the Universe) was surrounded by an unending stream of water, ruled by the god *Oceanus*. In the Buddhist approach, the world extends around Mount Meru, the centre of all the physical, metaphysical, and spiritual Universes. All these domains are separated from each other by seas, while the mountain itself is surrounded by a great ocean. And many, many other examples.

It seems that our forefathers regarded water more like a powerful concept rather than a simple physical substance. In other words, water wasn't the merely H_2O which we use today for our daily hydration, for cooking or doing dishes, to take a shower or flush the toilet.

For example, in the Bible, Jesus is described as the *"fountain of living water"* (Jeremiah 2:13), and in John 7:38 we read that anyone who believes in Him *"out of his belly shall flow rivers of living water"* (as translated in the *King James Version*), *"will have rivers of living water flowing from his heart"* (as narrated in the *International Standard Version*), or *"from his innermost being will flow rivers of living water"* (in the *New American Standard Bible*).

The "father of modern Chemistry" played a very important role in our current opinion regarding the life-giving substance us call "water". Antoine-Laurent de Lavoisier (1743 – 1794) by its name, tried, not even 300 years ago to develop own theories on combustion.

In one of his experiments, Lavoisier placed two gaseous substances in a glass balloon and ignited the mixture. He observed an explosion and the formation of a colourless gas, which rapidly condensed against the sides of the container, turning into a colourless liquid: Water.

The two gaseous substances used by Lavoisier in his experiment were previously known by the alchemists' as *"inflammable air"* and *"fire air"* (or *"vital air"*). Lavoisier changed the name of the *"inflammable air"* into "hydrogen" (the Greek *"water-former"*), while the *"vital air"* he termed it "oxygen", from the Greek *oxy-* (meaning *'sharp'*, *'keen'*, or *'acid'*), and *-genēs* (*producing*).

However, in my personal opinion, the previous names of these two gaseous substances were just fine. Hydrogen still remains the *"inflammable air"* because is known today as being very high in energy (used for this reason by NASA since the 1970s, to propel the space shuttles and other rockets into orbit). And as far as regarding oxygen, it is the main element that supports combustion (hence the *"fire air"* designation), and it is also the *"vital air"*, because a couple of minutes without oxygen could end our life (whereas a human being can go weeks without food and can survive days without drinking water).

Anyway, with his *Méthode de Nomenclature Chimique* (published in 1787), the "father of modern Chemistry" ended the ancient belief that water is a primordial element. He opened instead the path for another system of beliefs, in which the human being is the sole intelligence in a Universe filled with generic chemical substances.

Still, as previously mentioned, water is the only substance found in Nature that can change its visible states, from liquid to solid, or steam, in a blink of an eye (despite the fact that is composed of two chemical elements that are invisible to our physical senses). Even more, it's liquid phase represents the main constituent of every plant and animal cell, as well as the main component of the fluids of most living organisms.

And, if we really think about it, water has been with us since the beginning, even before we opened our eyes on this Blue Planet. We were born from the union of an ovum and a spermatozoon (which are made of more than 70% water), and we've developed all our major anatomical systems in our mother's womb, by swallowing and breathing the amniotic fluid (which is made up from 98% water).

As adult, all our major organs are composed of more than 70% water (the lungs - 84% water, the muscles and kidneys – up to 79% water, while the brain, the heart, the spinal cord, and the nerve trunks – all about 73% water), while the blood that carries the oxygen, the hormones, the nutrients and the waste products to and from our internal organs, is made of about 92% water.

Our entire existence, and all the activities we perform depend, one way or another, on water. The food and the drinks we consume, the homes we live in, the work we do, the clothes we wear, the way we are spending our free time, the ways we travel, and even our health – from the occasional sunburn to the common flu – they're all affected and influenced by the life-giving substance that we call "water".

Anyway, while I was "diving into the World of Water", I came upon another fascinating claim: that water has, somehow, the power to bring us joy and happiness, to give us strength and refreshment, to heal our bodies and take away sins.

This particular idea can be noticed not only at a careful reading of the ancient spiritual texts, but also at a close analysis of the traditions and rituals involving water (preserved and transmitted over millennia, for countless generations).

For example, in Christianity, Jesus began his ministry after being baptized in the waters of Jordan. By using the powers of water, he healed an infirm man at the pool at Bethesda (John 5:1-16) and a blind at the pool of Siloam (John 9:1-8). Actually, He performed many other works involving the water (calming the sea, turning water into wine, walking on water and so on), and in the Bible we even found His opinion about His works: *"Truly, truly, I say to you, he who believes in Me, the works that I do, he will do also; and greater works than these he will do;"* (John 14:12, NASB).

Water can be found at the centre of naming ceremony, ritual washing and ritual purification not only in Christianity, but in numerous spiritual traditions from all over the world: from Hindus to various Indigenous American rituals, in Judaism, Islam, Buddhism, Sikhism, Shinto, Taoism, Bahá'í Faith or the Rastafari Movement.

In fact, without being religious, almost every person is using water to wash his hands and his body when he feels dirty, or sprinkles his face with cold water when he feels tired, without even knowing that the ancient Hebrew people summarized these basic hygienical rules in five major rituals that involved the *"living water"*.

And, although washing our hands before we eat or when leaving the restroom are considered today basic hygienically rules, these practices weren't recognized by the medical community until late 19 century. As surprising it might sound, the Hungarian doctor Ignác Fülöp Semmelweis, was mocked and considered a lunatic just for suggesting that surgeons should wash their hands before surgical procedures. In 1865, his colleagues treacherously committed him to a mental asylum, where he died at the age of 47 (only 14 days after he was committed), because of an infection, after being beaten by the guards.

******

The purpose of this book is to shed a light upon our forefathers' claims regarding water, by comparing side-by-side, the ancient spiritual texts, traditions and rituals with the recent discoveries from various fields of science.

After all, we can't say that water belongs only to religion, nor that we find it only in Physics, Chemistry, Astronomy, Genetics or Biochemistry. I would say that it has instead, a History of its own[1], and it manifests its presence in ALL fields of knowledge.

Let's see if water has the power to bring joy and happiness, to heal and rejuvenate our bodies (as the ancient texts, traditions and rituals are claiming), or it's just a tasteless, odourless and nearly colourless substance, a mixture of two gaseous chemical elements, which just happens to be.

One thing is for sure: although our mainstream theory of Evolution propose that the modern *Homo Sapiens Sapiens* genus emerged over 200,000 years ago (and our pre-human ancestors walked on this Earth many million years before that), Water has been on this Blue Planet even longer, and was regarded by our forefathers more as a powerful concept, rather than a regular chemical substance.

And there's another thing. No matter how far we'd go back into our known history, we cannot find not even a single philosophic point of view or scientific domain in which the opinion of how we understand Nature and the Universe remained constant over a course of more than 500 years. By contrast, the spiritual teachings – in particular the traditions and rituals involving water – were transmitted from generation to generation, over centuries and millennia.

In the hope that I got your attention, let's begin, I would say, "swimming" (or "scuba-diving") into the "World of Water" and find out How WATER can help YOU change your LIFE!

---

[1] In one of my other books, titled *"Water's Healing Powers: Religion or Science?"* (self-published on December 5, 2017, thanks to Amazon services) I tried to gather as much information as possible regarding the "History of Water", including how accurate it respects (or, rather not) the well-established principles from Physics and Chemistry, among many other scientific fields.

CHAPTER 1. WATER IN THE BEGINNING OF EVERYTHING

Let's begin our journey in understanding the life-giving substance we call "Water" by taking a closer look at the physical evidences found in the ancient religious texts. And, let's start with probably the oldest written religious texts, a collection of carvings found in the Egyptian pyramids (dated to more than 4,000 years ago), known as the *Pyramid Texts*.

Most Egyptologists propose that the *Pyramid Texts* were reserved only for the Pharaoh, and, unlike other ancient Egyptian texts (such as the *Coffin Texts* or the *Book of the Dead*), they were primarily concerned with protecting the Pharaoh's remains, reanimating his body after death, and helping him ascend to the heavens.

According to the *Pyramid Texts*, the *"first event"* (*zep tepi*) took place in a dark, lifeless, everlasting and limitless mass of water (translated as *Nu, Nun,* or *Naunet*).

It was in these endless waters where *Atum,* associated with *Light, Life,* and the *Origin of Everything,* self-engendered as *Ra* (or *Rè*). Simultaneously with hatching out of his egg, *Atum* split himself into *Shu,* the God of the Wind and Air, *Tefnut,* the Goddess of Rain and Moisture, and their offspring: *Nut* (the Goddess of the Sky and Heavens) and her sibling, *Geb* (the God of the Earth).

The everlasting and limitless waters of *Nu* not only that represent the place where the ascending Pharaoh was born, but also the place that provides him protection against harmful deities. *Nu* allows the ascending Pharaoh to regenerate, by entering the *body of Osiris,* and return to the *first event* (*zep tepi*). The rituals found in the *Pyramid Texts* describe how the ascending Pharaoh escapes from the natural order, sees the gates of *Nu* opening, enters the waters of *Nu,* governs over those who are in *Nu,* and transforms into its limitless potential, *Atum.*

In another papyrus, known today as the Bremner-Rhind papyrus (dated roughly at 305 B.C.E.), we find *'The story of the Creation'* as it was supposed to be told by the god *Neb-er-tcher* (translated as the *'Lord to the uttermost limit'*). According to the text, *"Where and how Neb-er-tcher existed is not said, but it seems as if he was believed to have been an almighty and invisible power which filled all space. It seems also that a desire arose in him to create the world, and in order to do this he took upon himself the form of the god Khepera, who from first to last was regarded as the Creator, par excellence, among all the gods known to the Egyptians.*

When this transformation of Neb-er-tcher into Khepera took place the heavens and the earth had not been created, but there seem to have existed a vast mass of water, or world-ocean, called Nu, and it must have been in this that the transformation took place. In this celestial ocean were the germs of all the living things which afterwards took form in heaven and on earth, but they existed in a state of inertness and helplessness. Out of this ocean Khepera raised himself, and so passed from a state of passiveness and inertness into one of activity. When Khepera raised himself out of the ocean Nu, he found himself in vast empty space, wherein was nothing on which he could stand.

The second version of the legend says that Khepera gave being to himself by uttering his own name, and the first version states that he made use of words in providing himself with a place on which to stand. In other words, when Khepera was still a portion of the being of Neb-er-tcher, he spoke the word "Khepera," and Khepera came into being."[2] (emphasis added)

Many centuries after the Egyptian pyramids were built, another great culture arose in the south-eastern Mesopotamia (modern day Iraq), between the Tigris and Euphrates rivers.

Known today as the ancient Babylonians, their creation myth is one of the oldest in the world, and concerns the birth of the Gods and the Creation of the Universe and human beings.

The Babylonian Creation Myth, *Enûma Eliš*, is recorded in a collection of seven clay tablets, from where the modern name of *Seven Tablets of Creation* comes from. Most scholars date the tablets roughly between 18th and 16th centuries B.C.E., although the markings found of the tablets indicate that they are copies of a much older version of the myth.

According to *Enûma Eliš*, in the beginning, there was only undifferentiated water swirling in chaos. Out of this swirl, the waters divided into two principles: the male principle, represented by the sweet, fresh water (known as the Water-God *Apsu*), and the female principle, the salty, bitter water, the Goddess of the Ocean, *Tiamat*. Once differentiated, all the other younger Gods, and subsequently all beings, came into existence from the union between these two opposed principles.

> *"1. When the heavens above were yet unnamed,*
> *2. And the name of the earth beneath had not been recorded,*
> *3. Apsu, the oldest of beings, their progenitor,*
> *4. "Mummu" Tiamat, who bare each and all of them*
> *5. Their waters were merged into a single mass.*

---

[2] E.A. Wallis Budge, *Legends of the Gods. The Egyptian texts, edited with translations*, London, Kegan Paul, Trench and Trübner & Co. Ltd., 1912, pp. 5-6

6. *A field had not been measured; a marsh had not been searched out.*
7. *When the gods none was shining,*
8. *A name had not been recorded, a fate had not been fixed,*
9. *The gods came into being in the midst of them."*[3] (bold added)

Hinduism, another ancient system of beliefs (widely practiced even today), emerged along the Indus River Valley, as a fusion of various Indian cultures and traditions from the Himalayas to the Arabian Sea. It includes a diversity of ideas on spirituality and traditions, but has no governing body, no prophet(s) or any binding holy book, no ecclesiastical order and no unquestionable religious authorities. It is a matter of practice rather than of beliefs, founded more as a culture or a way of life.

Most scholars believe Hinduism started somewhere between 2300 B.C.E. and 1500 B.C.E., however, along with the excavations of the archaeological sites of the ancient Indus Valley civilizations (such as Mehrgarh, Mohenjo-Daro or Harappa), and because Hindus are still practicing some traditions which resemble to Neolithic people of India, modern scientists are considering the origins of Hinduism being as old as ancient Egypt or Mesopotamia.

Hindus philosophical concepts, creation myths, folktales and other traditional lore are recorded in many religious texts, yet, most Hindus revere the *Vedas* as the primary body of sacred literature. The *Vedas* represent a collection of verses and hymns that contains revelations received by ancient saints and sages, and for Hindus, these spiritual teachings transcend all time and don't have a beginning or an end.

One depiction of the initial conditions of the Creation of the Universe can be found in the in the *Rig Veda* (meaning *'Knowledge of the Verses'*), one of the oldest Hindu scriptures, and probably the world's oldest religious text in continued use:

"There was neither aught nor naught, nor air, nor sky beyond.
What covered all? Where rested all? In watery gulf profound?
Nor death was then, nor deathlessness, nor change of night and day.
The One breathed calmly, self-sustained; nought else beyond it lay.
Gloom, hid in gloom, existed first - one sea, eluding view.

[3] E.A. Wallis Budge, *The Babylonian Legends of the Creation and the Fight between Bel and the Dragons told by the Assyrian Tablets from Nineveh*, Department of Egyptian and Assyrian Antiquities, British Museum, June 1, 1921, pp. 31-32

That One, a void in chaos wrapt, by inward fervour grew.
Within it first arose desire, the primal germ of mind,
Which nothing with existence links, as sages searching find.
The kindling ray that shot across the dark and drear abyss –
Was it beneath? or high aloft? What bard can answer this?
There fecundating powers were found, and mighty forces strove –

A self-supporting mass beneath, and energy above.
Who knows, who ever told, from whence this vast creation rose?
No gods had then been born—who then can e'er the truth disclose?
Whence sprang this world, and whether framed by hand divine or no –
Its lord in heaven alone can tell, if even he can show.'[4] (bold added)

Following the traditions of their Indian forefathers, Buddhists consider the Universe infinite in time and space, filled with an infinite number of worlds like our own. Buddhists believe that one sees only what his karmic vision allows him to see, and the reality around us is just the product of one's mind.

Buddhism teaches that nothing is static or permanent, life is a continuous flow of interconnected moments. The nature of each moment is determined by what has gone before, just as one's next birth is determined by one's actions during this lifetime. In Buddhist approach, the soul of a person can go through repeatable cycles of births and re-births, governed by *karma* (meaning *'action'* and seen as the cause of one's particular destiny). As water goes through its hydrologic cycle, the soul of a person has the opportunity to experience life in different forms, being reborn as human, plant or animal body.

The concept of water is present throughout all Buddhist traditions, stories, beliefs, and meditations. It represents purity, clarity and calmness (with body, speech and mind), and many Buddhist references are made to flowing rivers as *'waters of life'*.

In Buddhist representation of the Universe there are six planes of existence, each associated with one of the six main negative emotions. The *Narakas* – the hell plain of existence – is associated with anger, the *Pretas* (or the hungry ghosts), is related to greed, the animal realm (*Tiryaks*) is associated with ignorance. *Manusyas* (or humans) are associated with desire, *Asuras* (the demigods' realm of existence) is identified with jealousy, while the *Devas* (the gods) are associated with pride.

---

[4] William Joseph Wilkins, *"Hindu Mythology, Vedic and Purānic"*, Thacker, Spink & Company, 1882, pg. 243.

Above these realms of desire there are the realms of form (*rupa-dhatu*) and the even higher realm of formlessness (*arupa-dhatu*). All these domains (*gatis*) are separated from each other by seas, and surrounded by a great ocean.

Another religious belief that continued, in one form or another, from ancient times to present days, is the monotheistic religion of Judaism. Although the belief in one God was a minor view at the time when Judaism emerged, Hebrew's basic principles became dominant nowadays, because of the influence upon powerful religions of Christianity and Islam.

According to most scholars, Judaism was established in the ancient eastern region of Canaan, the area inhabited by the Israelites between the Jordan River and the Mediterranean (now Israel and Palestinian territories). However, Judaism's emergence date remains unclear. The beginning of the Israelites' religion is considered to have begun along with the Covenant between God and Abraham *Avinu* (*'our Father Abraham'*), who plays a prominent role as an example of faith in Judaism. In Christianity, Abram is referred to as *'our Father in Faith'* by the Roman Catholic Church, while in Islam, 'Ibrāhīm is seen as a link in the chain of prophets that began with Adam and culminated with Muhammad.

The Tanakh – as the Bible of the Hebrews and their Jewish descendants down to the present – has been perhaps the most decisive single factor in the preservation of the Jews as a cultural entity and Judaism as a religion. Narrated in the Book of Bereshit (meaning *'In the Beginning'*), the process of creation of Heaven and the Earth is depicted as follows:

"¹When God began to create heaven and earth, **²and the earth then was welter and waste and darkness over the deep and God's breath hovering over the waters,** *³God said, "Let there be light." And there was light. ⁴And God saw the light, that is was good, and God divided the light from the darkness. ⁵And God called the light Day, and the darkness He called Night. And it was the evening and it was the morning, first day. ⁶And God said,* **"Let there be a vault in the midst of the waters, and let it divide water from water."** *⁷And God made the vault and it divided the water beneath the vault from the water above the vault, and so it was. ⁸**And God called the vault Heavens,** and it was the evening and it was the morning, second day. ⁹And God said,* **"Let the waters under the heavens be gathered in one place so that the dry land will appear",** *and so it was. ¹⁰**And God called the dry land Earth and the gathering of waters He called Seas, and God saw that it was good."***⁵ (emphasis added)

---

⁵ Robert Alter, *The Hebrew Bible: A Translation with Commentary*, W. W. Norton & Company, Kindle edition (2018), Chapter 1.

Over the centuries, the Hebrew Tanakh become the textual source for the Christian Old Testament. Most of the Bibles around the world have as a source the *King James Version,* KJV (or *King James Bible,* KJB), a translation made over a period of 7 years (between 1604-1611), by a group of 47 members of the Church of England.

The original KJV translation contained 39 books of the Old Testament, 27 books of the New Testament, plus another 14 books of the Apocrypha (meaning *"things that are secret, hidden"*). The apocryphal books are covering a period of about 400 years, also known as the *'Silent 400 years',* a gap of time between the Hebrew Bible and the Christian New Testament (roughly between the ministry of Malachi in c. 420 B.C.E. and the appearance of John the Baptist in the early 1st century C.E.).

Despite its many translations and interpretations available, the Bible was (and remains) one of the most inspirational books for many categories of people. It holds the Guinness World Records for the *Oldest mechanically printed book* and *Best-selling book of non-fiction,* and helps countless individuals, from various social categories, to change their lives, to become more loving, humble, grateful, selflessness and compassionate.

When it comes about water, in the KJV Book of Genesis we find basically the same depiction of the initial Creation as in the Hebrew Book of Bereshit:

"¶ In the beginning God created the heaven and the earth.
² And the earth was without form, and void; **and darkness was upon the face**
of the deep. And the Spirit of God moved upon the face of the waters.
³ And God said, Let there be light: and there was light.
⁴ And God saw the light, that it was good: and God divided the light from the darkness.
⁵ And God called the light Day, and the darkness he called Night. And the evening and the morning were the first day.
⁶ And God said, **Let there be a firmament in the midst of the waters,**
and let it divide the waters from the waters.
⁷ And God made the firmament, **and divided the waters which were under**
the firmament from the waters which were above the firmament: *and it was so.*
⁸ And God called the firmament Heaven. And the evening and the morning were the second day.
⁹ And God said, **Let the waters under the heaven be gathered together**
unto one place, *and let the dry land appear: and it was so.*
¹⁰ And God called the dry land Earth; and the gathering together of the waters called He Seas: and God saw that it was good." (Genesis 1:10, KJV, bold added)

As previously mentioned, the original KJB contained 14 apocryphal books. These old manuscripts are slowly rediscovered and translated, yet, in all the versions, we can find water playing a prominent role in the beginning of the Creation. For example, in the surviving fragments of the *Sibylline Oracles* (closely guarded oracular scrolls written by the Sibylls prophetic priestesses during the Etruscan and early Roman Era, as far back as the 6th century B.C.E.), we find in the beginning of the First Book (verses 10-25), the description of the creation of the Earth and man:

"10 The King most high, who brought into existence
The whole world, saying, "Let there be," and there was.
For he the earth established, placing it
Round about Tartarus[6], and he himself
Gave the sweet light; he raised the heaven on high,

15 **Spread out the gleaming sea, and crowned the sky**
With an abundance of bright-shining stars,
And decked the earth with plants, and mingled sea
With rivers, and the air with zephyrs mixed
And watery clouds; and then, another race

20 Appointing, he gave fishes to the seas
And birds unto the winds, and to the woods
The beasts of shaggy neck, and snakes that crawl,
And all things which now on the earth appear.
These by his word he made, and every thing."[7] (bold added)

---

[6] *Tartarus* represented a vast mass of water within the Earth, mentioned in the writings of the Greek poet Homer (c. 800 B.C.E. – c. 701 B.C.E.), Thales of Miletus (c. 620 B.C.E. – c. 546 B.C.E.) and Plato (427 – 347 B.C.E.).
Aristotle (384 – 322 B.C.E.) wrote in his *Meteorologica* (c.350 B.C.E.) that *"There it is said that the earth is pierced by intercommunicating channels and that the original head and source of all waters is what is called Tartarus a mass of water about the centre, from which all waters, flowing and standing, are derived. This primary and original water is always surging to and fro, and so it causes the rivers to flow on this side of the earth's centre and on that; for it has no fixed seat but is always oscillating about the centre. Its motion up and down is what fills rivers. Many of these form lakes in various places (our sea is an instance of one of these), but all of them come round again in a circle to the original source of their flow, many at the same point, but some at a point opposite to that from which they issued; for instance, if they started from the other side of the earth s centre, they might return from this side of it. They descend only as far as the centre, for after that all motion is upwards. Water gets its tastes and colours from the kind of earth the rivers happened to flow through."* [The Works of Aristotle, translated into English under the editorship of W.D. Ross, Volume III: *Meteorologica*, by E.W. Webster, first edition 1931, reprinted at the University Press, Oxford, 1968, Book II.2, 355b-356a]
[7] Milton S. Terry, *The Sibylline Oracles translated from the Greek into English blank verse*, New York: Eaton & Mains, Cincinnati: Curts & Jennings, 1899

In Judaism and Christianity, water plays a major role in the process of Creation. Not only that *"in the beginning"* God created *"a firmament in the midst of the waters"* and divided *"the waters from the water"*, but all the plants and herbs grew only after a mist went up *"from the earth, and watered the whole face of the ground"* (Genesis 2:5-6). Adam, the first man, was placed in the Garden of Eden, where *"a river flowed out of Eden to water the garden, and there it divided and became four rivers"* (Genesis 2:10 ESV).[8]

The initial creation of the Earth *"out of water"* is also mentioned in the New Testament (2 Peter 3:5-6): *"For they deliberately overlook this fact, that the heavens existed long ago, and **the earth was formed out of water and through water by the word of God**, and that by means of these the world that then existed was deluged with water and perished."*

As in all the other ancient religious beliefs, in Islam (the third Abrahamic religion, and the second-largest religion in the world after Christianity), water represents the primary substance on which *"the throne of His almightiness has rested"*.
"And He it is who has created the heavens and the earth in six aeons; and [ever since He has willed to create life,] the throne of His almightiness has rested upon water" (The Qur'an, *Hud* 11:7, bold added).

"And it is God who has created all animals out of water; *and [He has willed that] among them are such as crawl on their bellies, and such as walk on two legs, and such as walk on four. God creates what He will: for, verily, God has the power to will anything."* (The Qur'an, *An-Nur* 24.45, bold added).

"And He it is who out of this [very] water has created man, *and has endowed him with [the consciousness of] descent and marriage-tie for thy Sustainer is ever infinite in His power* (The Qur'an, *Al-Furqan* 25.54, bold added).

"ARE, THEN, they who are bent on denying the truth not aware that the heavens and the earth were [once] one single entity, which We then parted asunder? and [that] We made out of water every living thing?" (The Qur'an, *Al-Anbiya* 21.30, bold added)

Now, let's see if there's a hidden message encrypted in all these ancient texts, by switching from religion to our modern scientific understanding regarding the formation of the Universe and the emergence of life.

---

[8] In the KJV version, the river which flowed out of Eden divided into "four heads", yet, at a further reading of the text, we find at Genesis 2:11-14 the description of the "heads": Pison (*"which compasseth the whole land of Havilah"*), Gihon (*"that compasseth the whole land of Ethiopia"*), Hiddekel (*"which goeth toward the east of Assyria"*) and *"the fourth river is Euphrates"*.

According to the most prevalent theory of the formation of our Universe (known as the Big Bang theory), all the space, time, matter and energy, emerged circa 13.8 billion years ago, from an unimaginably hot, dense point. All four main forces that are ruling the visible Universe (gravity, electromagnetism, the weak and strong forces) and the invisible universe (vacuum energy/space energy and dark energy), were united into a single force.

The primordial singularity started to expand, faster than the speed of light, and, in a matter 10^{-36} seconds (meaning a trillionth of a trillionth of a trillionth of a second), the Universe filled with a hot, dense plasma, while the matter and the antimatter annihilated each other and created light.

Until this point, we might say that the ancient religious texts are not so far from the truth. In all of them, in the beginning, there was a force, a spirit, or some sort of primordial energy, while Light was separated from the Dark, Day from the Night, or Good from Evil.

Modern cosmologists, astronomers and theoretical physicists propose that as the singularity started to expand, the space cooled enough to allow the first particles to form, giving birth to deuterium (^{2}D), an isotope of the hydrogen.

During the nucleogenesis of the initial expansion, only the first four lightest elements from the Periodic Table of the Elements were formed: hydrogen, helium and trace amounts of lithium and beryllium. All the other chemical elements known today emerged from nuclear reactions in stars and in huge stellar explosions known as supernovae.

I will not make now a throughout description of the Big Bang theory, or its nucleosynthesis (though I encourage everyone interested in how the chemical elements formed to do so), I will focus instead of the original quest: Could it be possible to have existed a *vast mass of water* (as all the ancient texts propose) before our Earth and all the life, came into existence?

According to our current scientific understanding, hydrogen is the lightest, simplest, and most abundant chemical element in the visible Universe. As already mentioned in the preface, the term was coined by Antoine-Laurent de Lavoisier, and basically means *water former*.

However, hydrogen is present not only in water, but in all organic compounds and living organisms. It accounts for up to 75% of normal matter by mass and over 90% by the number of atoms, holding the first position in the Periodic Table of the Elements, because of its simplest structure and lowest density among all the other chemical elements.

Scientists agree that without the existence of the nuclear forces (the crucial forces for the existence of matter as we know it), there would be no nuclei, except for individual protons and neutrons. The neutrons would decay radioactively and disappear in a short time, while the protons would become in their turn the nuclei of hydrogen atoms. Thus, the only matter that would exist would be composed of the *'water former'*, hydrogen.

Oxygen, the second water component, was known by alchemists since antiquity as *'fire air'* or *'vital air'*, due to the fact that is the main chemical element that supports combustion, and represents the single most vital element for most of the Earth's life. For example, as human beings, we could survive for weeks without carbon in foodstuffs, or we could go days without drinking water. Yet, just a couple of minutes without the *'vital air'* (oxygen) could end our life.

Although we find oxygen on the 8th position in the Periodic Table of the Elements (two positions behind carbon, and way behind the noble gases formed in the initial 'Big Bang'), it represents the third-most chemical element in the Universe, after hydrogen and helium. Oxygen also accounts for almost half of the mass of the Earth's crust, two-thirds of the mass of the human body and makes up nearly 21% of the Earth's atmosphere.

Again, we might say that the ancient texts and manuscripts are holding some water. Hydrogen is the most abundant chemical element in the known visible Universe, while oxygen is the third (despite its atomic number 8, and that, according to nucleosynthesis, was produced much later than other elements). These two colourless, odourless and tasteless chemical elements existed in the Universe long before our Earth came into existence (circa 4.5 billion years ago, as astronomers propose).

Moreover, these two gaseous substances (thus invisible to our physical senses), not only that are giving birth to a visible substance, but water is THE ONLY substance found in Nature that has the ability to become visible in three different phases: liquid, solid (as ice or snow) and vapor (steam).

Now, if we take into the consideration the forces that govern our visible world (gravity, electromagnetism and the nuclear forces), and the invisible world (vacuum energy/zero-point energy or space energy, dark energy and so on), we might say that the ancient texts are not so far from the truth with their claims that in the beginning, an *"invisible force"*, a *"spirit"* was *"hovering over the faces of the water"*, divided *"the waters from the water"*, and founded the Earth upon waters.

This highest universal principle, force or spirit, which manifests its presence in all seeing and unseeing things, has different names in various cultures. In the Hebrew tradition, it is known as *Ruach* (רוּחַ), meaning *"wind"*, *"breath"*, or *"spirit"*. In the early Western system of Philosophy, it was known as *Ether*. In Christianity, the *Holy Spirit*. In Hindu traditions it is referred to as *Brahman* (the formless form of energy which manifest in every person as

Atman), *Kundalini* (the primal energy and consciousness which has been coiled at the base of the spine since birth), *Shakti* (the dynamic forces that are moving through the entire Universe), or *Prana*, the life force, or vital principle that comprises all cosmic energy, permeating the Universe on all levels. In the Chinese beliefs it is described as *Qi* or *Ch'I*, the energy flow that forms part of any living thing. In Japanese beliefs, its counterpart is known as *Ki*, *Reiki* or *Hado*. And so on.

Regarding how water ended up on our Blue Planet, covering more than 70% of its surface with splendid oceans, seas, lake and rivers, scientists don't have yet a definitive answer. Some propose that Earth must have inherited much of its water from the cloud of gas from which the Sun was born, others suggest that water is a product of the planet-forming process (and planets are born with liquid water oceans), while others theorize that water came much later, from collisions with wet comets and asteroids.

Still, they all agree on one thing: Water existed on this Blue Planet long before any other form of life came into existence.

And when it comes about the emergence of life, we encounter the same long, continuous debate among scientists. There are many theories of the origins of life, but since it's hard to prove or disapprove them, there's no fully accepted theory. While some scientists think they had figured out approximately _when_ life first appeared on Earth, they are still far from answering _how_ it appeared.

They all agree, however, that we need water in order to survive, there's life as we know it wherever there is water on Earth. Moreover, water had something to do, one way or another, with the emergence of life.

As far as concerning the human body, all scientists agree that we are "water machines", designed to run primarily on water and minerals. And that's just because water performs in our bodies many crucial functions. For example, it is the most vital nutrient for the life of every cell, allowing body cells to grow, reproduce and survive, acting first as a building material.

If we would zoom inside any form of plant or animal life, we'll see thousands, millions, and even trillions of cells, which in their turn form internal organs, or shoot and root systems. Inside these tiny *building blocks of life* (as we often refer to the cells), we'll find an entire world, as amazing as the one we see around us.

Although made mostly of water, every cell has its own respiratory system, digestive, excretory, endocrine, integumentary, nervous, reproductive and immune system. The normal functioning of all these systems, as well as the cell's health and ability to reproduce, are strictly related to its water content.

Water is known as the *universal solvent*, because it can dissolve or dissociate more particles than any other liquid. This is a crucial property without which life as we know would not exist. Water carries, wherever it goes – through air, on land, deep underground and inside every single living organism –, valuable chemicals, minerals and nutrients (and also microplastics and other harmful chemical elements).

In Physics and Fluid Mechanics we encounter a process called osmosis. In medicine we know it as dialysis, and the term refers to water's ability to move freely through a membrane, from the side of the membrane with a high concentration of water, to the side with a low concentration of water. For example, if we submerge a cell in saltwater, water molecules will move out of the cell. Conversely, when submerged in freshwater, water molecules will move into the cell.

Both the above phenomena are encountered all around in Nature, regardless that we are talking about humans, animals or plants' stem or root. Water's ability to move freely through permeable membranes plays a crucial role in all life on Earth, because in every living thing, most biological membranes are more permeable to water than to ions or other solutes. Since water molecules are the most abundant in cells, because of the phenomenon of osmotic flow, the cells maintain a constant chemical environment.

In our bodies, water dissolves the substances that enter from the food and drink we consume and the air we breathe. Due to the process of osmosis, it passes easily through the cell's membrane, carrying the oxygen, minerals and nutrients required for the regular functioning and nourishment of every single cell. Through our bloodstream transports the oxygen needed to survive, and removes all the unnecessary substances, through sweat, bodily waste and urine. It helps our brain to manufacture hormones and neurotransmitters, acts as a shock absorber for the brain, the spinal cord, and surrounds the foetus in the amniotic sac, during pregnancy. Moistens tissues such as those in the mouth, nose, eyes and lungs, forms saliva, lubricates and cushions joints. And many, many other functions.

* * * * * *

"Biology has forgotten water or never even thought of it."
Dr. Albert Szent-Gyorgyi (1893 – 1986),
laureate of the Nobel Prize in Physiology or Medicine in 1937

* * * * * *

If we really think about it, water has been with us from the beginning. We were born from the union of a woman's ovum (the "egg cell", which has a water content of over 70%) and a male's spermatozoon, which density, and also its quality, depends almost entirely of its water content.

We're spending our first 38-40 weeks in our mother's womb, where we are surrounded by the amniotic fluid. In this nice, warm, watery environment, we develop all major anatomical systems by swallowing and breathing the content of the amniotic fluid, which is made up from 98% water.

In our foetus stage, we are made up by 94% water and even as adults, all our major organs consist of over 50% water. Our lungs are about 84% water, while the brain, the heart, the spinal cord, and the nerve trunks – all about 73% water. Our muscles and kidneys are made up of 79% water, our skin has 65% water, and even our bones are 31% watery. To and from our internal organs, the oxygen, the hormones, the nutrients and the waste products are carried by the blood, which is made of about 92% water.

And, even more, if we would zoom inside a human body, starting from the molecular level, we'll see an ocean of 99% hydrogen and oxygen molecules. It's like picturing ourselves inside a cell, and start counting until a hundred: we would say "water"…, "water"…, "water"… for 99 times, and one time out of a hundred we would say "protein"…, "DNA"…, "calcium"…or "magnesium".

However, we're not the only form of life on this Blue Planet. There are an estimate of 8.7 million plant and animal species living on Earth, from which we identified and described only about 14% of land species and about 9% of sea species.

At the same time, the ancient religious texts narrate that water is the source of every form of life, plant or animal.

Let's see if this might be true, by making another journey, this time in the fields of Genetics and Biochemistry.

Before we start, I would like to mention that I'm aware that these two branches of science are not amongst the favourite lectures for many readers, so I will try not to go into too extensive details. As before, we'll just track the chemical elements, and in particular the *water former* (hydrogen) and the *vital air* (oxygen).

According to our current scientific understanding, most living systems contain only six different chemical elements: hydrogen (H), carbon (C), nitrogen (N), phosphorus (P), oxygen (O), and sulphur (S), while the DNA and mRNA sequences consists of only five chemical elements: C, O, H, N and P.

I'm sure that many of you are familiar with the twisted ladder shaped DNA molecule. This double helix shape (as scientists refer to the DNA's twisted ladder) contains all the biological instructions that make each species unique, as well as the instructions needed for every living organism to develop, survive, and reproduce.

Now, the DNA twisted ladder has two alternating strands (sugar molecules and phosphate groups), while the rungs of the ladder are made of nitrogenous bases, with hydrogen bonds between them.

From Genetics perspective, the nitrogenous bases are formed of four building blocks – known as adenine (A), thymine (T), guanine (G) and cytosine (C) –, and represent the compounds which make up organisms' genes. The order, or sequence of the nitrogen bases determines what biological instructions are contained in a strand of DNA. For example, for blue eyes, the sequence might be ATCGTT, while ATCGCT might instruct for brown eyes.

As an interesting fact, in the base pairing (also called nucleotide pairing), A will always pair with T, and C will always pair with G. And since I mentioned this, let me mention a couple more (I might say interesting) facts about DNA. You might call it a little break from the rigorous Genetics class (or getting out of the water for a second).

Scientists discovered that the DNA is 1.8 meters long, or about 6 feet. Yet, it can squeeze into a tiny space of just 0.09 micrometres, meaning 1,000 times smaller than a millimetre (one millimetre is about 0.039 inches, so do the math).

Now, if we think that there are trillions of cells in our bodies, if we could take out all the DNA from the cells and stretch it, we could encircle our entire Solar System, twice!

In the human genome, there are about 3 billion base pairs, meaning 3,000,000,000 different combinations of A, T, G and C. However, out of these 3 billion, only 0.1% are unique to one person. In other words, no matter where we were born on this Blue Planet, what colour is our skin, what language we speak, or what political or religious beliefs we have, OUR DNA IS MORE 99.9% IDENTICAL THAN DIFFERENT!

Moreover, about 8% of what we think of as our "human" DNA, actually comes from viruses that first infected our ancestors hundreds of thousands of years ago. This means we carry around in our DNA the dormant form of all our ancestors' viruses.

When it comes about life on this Blue Planet, we share about 99% DNA with the chimpanzees, but also with their favourite food, the banana (over 50%).

If we would take a peek inside the human DNA, we'll see thousands of genes (some 20,000 to 25,000, according to geneticists). Although this number might sound impressive, those genes represent only about 2% of our DNA; the rest of 98% (as surprisingly it might sound) is considered "junk" DNA. In its turn, from that itty-bitty 2%, containing thousands of genes, only 95 of them, known as imprinted genes, are coming from one of our parents and are subject to parent-of-origin effect. That's right, 95 genes, out of thousands of genes, out of 2% of our DNA.

We also share 98% of our genes with the chimpanzees and 92% with mice and rats (used for this reason in laboratory experiments for testing future human drugs); we share 90% of the genes with cats, who in their turn, have similar genes with dogs (about 82%), with chimpanzees (79%), and also with rats and mice (about 67-69%). We also share 80% of our genes with cows, 60% with chicken and 60% with the common fruit fly, drosophila melanogaster. We even share 26% of our genes with the yeast, the classic bread (or pizza) dough, because scientists found that we share a common ancestor.

And, last but not least, our partners can "smell" the DNA. Studies of kissing shown that women are more attracted to the scent of a man with a different genetic code that her own.

Now, let's go back to Genetics, inside the cell, (or let's say we go back into the water, since the content of a cell is almost entirely made of water), and see what's happening with the DNA in a regular cell function.

Except cellular division, when DNA gets in its tiny, compact, chromosome form, DNA's twisted ladder has to stretch, to unwind, so it can be read, replicated, or repaired. In fact, because both normal metabolic activities and environmental factors, DNA damage in our cells occurs at a rate of 10,000 to 1,000,000 molecular lesions per cell per day.

The watery environment that we call "cell" identifies the damaged DNA, and tries to repair it. A cell's ability to repair its DNA depends on many factors, including cell type, its age, and its extracellular environment (which again, is mostly water).

A cell that has accumulated a large amount of DNA damage, or one that can no longer repair the damage incurred to its DNA, enters one of three states: either becomes dormant, it either suicides (known in Genetics as apoptosis or programmed cell death), or, third, starts an unregulated cell division, which can lead to the formations of tumours.

Now, scientists were curious about what holds together the strands and the rungs of the DNA ladder, and, most recently, the prevailing theory was that the base pairs are held together by the hydrogen bonds. Yet, new scientific findings reveal that the DNA molecules' nitrogen bases have a hydrophobic interior, in an environment consisting mainly of water. Furthermore, scientists observed that the DNA molecules' characteristic spiral form starts to unravel when it reaches the borderline between hydrophilic and hydrophobic environments.

To remember better the difference between these two terms (hydrophobic and hydrophilic), you can access that particular DNA sequence that contains your ancient Greek heritage and reminds you that in Greek *'philos'* means love, while *'phobos'* means fear (or you can just Google it). So basically, when we are talking about water's solubility (or environment) we can say that hydrophilic substances are "water loving", while hydrophobic are "water fearing" substances.

"Cells want to protect their DNA, and not expose it to hydrophobic environments, which can sometimes contain harmful molecules" says one of the researchers involved in the study. *"But at the same time, the cells' DNA needs to open up in order to be used. We believe that the cell keeps its DNA in a water solution most of the time, but as soon as a cell wants to do something with its DNA, like read, copy or repair it, it exposes the DNA to a hydrophobic environment."*[9]

Wait, what!? Before creating something out of the DNA, the cell keeps its DNA in a water solution most of the time? And only when the cell wants to read, copy or repair its DNA, takes it out of the water?

It's almost like we started reading the book from the beginning, and we're reading in some, God knows what ancient manuscript, that everything comes out from water and water is in the beginning of everything (ok, the simplified version, without so many scientific, complex terms).

So far so good, it's pretty clear that water has a crucial importance at the molecular level. Now, bear with me, and let's switch from Genetics to Biochemistry, and let's zoom from the molecular level to the planetary level.

As I already mentioned, the DNA is comprised of only five chemical elements: carbon, oxygen, hydrogen, nitrogen and phosphorus. All these chemical elements undergo in Nature a continuous cycle, without which life as we know would not exist.

We have, of course, the well-known H_2O cycle: water goes up in the sky, gathers into clouds, and comes back as rain or snow, goes underground and up again, changing its states from liquid to solid (ice) and gas (vapour), in a blink of an eye. This cycle is crucial for all life and ecosystems on our Blue Planet.

However, besides the water cycle, we also have a carbon cycle, a nitrogen cycle, and, as main component of DNA, the phosphorus cycle.

Let's begin with the carbon cycle, since it represents the basic building block for all forms of life on Earth (remember how many times you heard that we are carbon-based life forms). Not only that carbon accounts for about

---

[9] *Scientists Were Wrong About DNA – It Is Actually Held Together by Hydrophobic Forces*, Chalmers University of Technology, published on SciTechDaily, September 22, 2019

18% of the human body, but it can also be found in all living organisms as a key component of carbohydrates (sugars and starches), lipids (fats and oils), proteins and nucleic acids (DNA and RNA).

As a short parenthesis, the so-feared "carbs" from Nutrition (or its scientific term, carbohydrates) represent the main source of energy for both plants and animals. In Biology we refer to the carbohydrates as saccharides (a group that includes sugars, starch and cellulose), and consist only of carbon, hydrogen and oxygen, where the *water former* hydrogen is the most abundant.

For our chemists' and mathematicians' friends, the carbohydrates empirical formula looks something like this: $C_m(H_2O)_n$ (where m could differ from n).

As a matter of fact, even glucose, the most important source of energy for cellular respiration (stored in plants as starch and in animals as glycogen) is comprised only of hydrogen, carbon and oxygen, where hydrogen is the most abundant. But let's not digress and let's return to the carbon cycle.

On our Blue Planet, we find carbon abundantly in Earth's atmosphere in the form of carbon dioxide (CO_2), and deep underground, in the form of fossil fuels (such as oil, coal and natural gas), and methane (CH_4). As another interesting fact (who's counting them), CO_2 can dissolve in water 200 times more easily than oxygen (thank you, Coca-Cola and Pepsi).

Now, I am sure everybody heard about photosynthesis. It is a crucial process in the carbon cycle and is played by the plant life. During photosynthesis, the plants convert the CO_2 from the atmosphere, and, with the help of energy from the Sun and water drawn up from the roots, they generate carbohydrates as a main product, and oxygen as a by-product. At the same time, CO_2 represents the by-product of animals and humans (including their industrial and domestic activities).

In Chemistry, the general formula of the process of photosynthesis looks like this: $CO_2 + 2H_2O + photons \rightarrow [CH_2O] + O_2 + H_2O$ (meaning that carbon dioxide + water + light energy $\rightarrow$ carbohydrate + oxygen + water).

In other words, we might say that the CO_2, the by-product of animals and humans, is "inhaled" by the plants in order to produce their main source of energy (carbohydrates), while the by-product of plant activities is "inhaled" by the animal life in order to survive. Water is…well…just H_2O in Chemistry, on the both sides of the formula (except that the plants use "2x" water for converting the carbon dioxide into carbohydrates).

Now, let's track another DNA component, the nitrogen. It accounts for about 78% of the Earth's atmosphere (yes, over three times the amount of *vital air*, oxygen) and is essential to all forms of life. This is just because nitrogen is the basic ingredient in amino-acids, that make up all proteins. Now, as opposed to the term "protein" encountered in the popular language (or found on various food labels), in Biology protein refers to complex molecules that perform most of the work in the cells and are required for the structure, function and regulation of the body's tissues and organs. The term "protein" comprises not only structural components (such as muscle, tissue and organs), but also enzymes, antibodies and hormones essential for the functioning of all living things.

Let's see where the nitrogen goes around with respect to our Blue Planet. Although we find it very abundant in the atmosphere as diatomic nitrogen gas (N_2), nitrogen is extremely stable, and conversion to other forms requires a great amount of energy. Not going into too many details here, long story short, in Nature the nitrogen cycle follows five steps: fixation, nitrification, assimilation, ammonification and denitrification.

The first step, fixation, takes place in the absence of oxygen, when nitrogen is converted into NH_3/NH_4+ by a small group of bacteria and cyanobacteria. The second step (nitrification) requires the presence of oxygen, and NH_3/NH_4+ is converted into NO_3- (and further, another soil bacterium oxidizes NO_2- to NO_3-).

During the third step (assimilation), plants and animals incorporate the NO_3- and NH_3 formed through nitrification and fixation. Assimilation, by the way, produces the largest quantities of organic nitrogen (including proteins, amino acids, and nucleic acids).

In the fourth step (ammonification), the organic nitrogen is converted back to ammonia (NH_3), which is released to the environment to become available for either nitrification or assimilation. And, finally, during the fifth step, NO_3- is reduced back to gaseous N_2 by anaerobic bacteria. This process can occur only deep in the soil, where there is little to no atmospheric oxygen. The nitrogen gas (N_2) is released back into the atmosphere, and the cycle goes on and on.

Ok, the above simplified cycle is just what we learn in the Biochemistry class (with a bunch of chemical formulas on top). If we would attend some class of environmental science, we'll probably learn that our Earth's chemical balance changed significantly during the last century, and in fact, since the beginning of the Industrial Revolution.

We increased the burning of fossil fuels, we built more than 60,000 power generation plants all over the world, and we use, God knows how many, internal combustion engines (there's an estimate of more than a billion cars traveling on the roads, and we're not counting here the water-vehicles, locomotives, aircrafts, lawnmowers, string trimmers, chain saws, leaf-blowers, pressure washers, snowmobiles, jet skis, outboard motors, mopeds, motorcycles and so on).

Even more, until the discovery in the early 1900s of the Haber-Bosch process (the artificial nitrogen fixation process and the main industrial procedure for the production of ammonia today), the naturally occurring sources of reactive nitrogen for food production were manure and guano. Since then, because of the extensive use of artificial nitrogen fertilizers, the level of nitrogen oxides in the atmosphere increased dramatically (and if we're piling up the massive deforestations, and the burning of fossil fuels, even the levels of carbon dioxide exploded), having a huge impact on all ecosystems, including Earth's atmosphere, water and soil quality.

In fact, recent scientific studies show that humans create over two times as much reactive nitrogen as the rest of our Blue Planet, causing profound environmental impacts (including smog, acid rain, forest dieback, coastal 'dead zones', stratospheric ozone depletion, and increase greenhouse gases) and affecting human health (through respiratory diseases, increasing risk for birth defects and many others).

It's sad, but it is what it is, and it's up to us and to our future generations to balance the things (so you can help by spreading the knowledge and recommend this book to all your beloved ones).

Back to Biochemistry, there's one more chemical component of the DNA left. Phosphorus, as well as the phosphorus-based compounds, is found usually in solid form, at the typical ranges of temperatures and pressure found in Nature. Thus, phosphorus does not enter the atmosphere. It remains mostly on land, and in rock and soil minerals. Still, it is an essential nutrient for plants and animals, and occurs most abundantly as part of the orthophosphate ion (PO_4^{3-}).

I will not overburden you by making a detailed presentation of the chemical reactions that occur in the above cycles, instead I'll make a rather intriguing observation: in ALL the cycles (the water cycle, the nitrogen cycle and the carbon cycle), the main role is played by ONLY TWO components: hydrogen (the *water former*), and oxygen (former known as *vital air* or *fire air*), in which the *water former* is the key component. (you can look it up yourselves, if you don't believe me).

* * * * * *

"Water is the mater and matrix, mother and medium of life."
Dr. Albert Szent-Gyorgyi (1893 – 1986), Nobel Prize in Physiology or Medicine – 1937

* * * * * *

27

So far, it seems that the ancient religious texts are not just simple fairy-tales. Indeed, no matter from what scientific point of view we look at the water, we might say that in the beginning there was only water and everything comes from water.

Now let's move on to the second claim encountered in all the traditions around the world, that water has the ability to bring joy and happiness, heal and rejuvenate our bodies.

For example, in the ancient Egyptian beliefs, the limitless waters of *Nu* represented not only the place where the ascending Pharaoh was born but also the place that allows him to regenerate, transforming into its limitless potential, *Atum*. In Chinese beliefs, water represents a symbol that can bring a greater and purer state of existence, removing what has soiled the quality of life. For Hindus all waters are sacred, being in the beginning, centre and end of this universe (and the human life within it). In Buddhist traditions, water symbolizes purity, clarity and calmness (with body, speech and mind). In Judaism, all natural bodies of water are treated as *living water* in the ritual of *mikveh*, symbolizing the presence of God through flow, loving, kindness, abundance and prosperity. In Christianity, God and Jesus are described as *"fountains of living water"*, while any person who believes in the Scriptures, *"out of his heart will flow rivers of living water"*. In many Christian churches, we find the holy water (water that has been previously blessed by a priest), used to protect persons, objects or places, from evil. And many other examples.

Perhaps, as in the previous case, the ancient texts might be true. But if indeed, water has the power to heal our bodies, how is this possible?

Can it be proven by our modern science, and it is something that we can understand and apply in our daily life? Or are just simple bed-time stories?

CHAPTER 2. THE MEMORY OF WATER

The majority believes that science has figured out everything there is to be known about water, and regards it merely as a regular chemical substance, having the well-known H_20 chemical formula. Still, water holds many mysteries even for our modern researchers, and has been a topic of interest for many areas of science.

For example, back in the 1960s, the Director of the Molecular Biology Department of the Pennsylvania Hospital, Dr. Gilbert Ling, discovered that water found in the human cells are ordered similar to crystals found in ice, in the way that it pushes out from the crystal any impurities.

In 1965, he published a paper in which he argued that the *"living cells, as a rule, contain 15 to 25 percent proteins and 75 to 85 percent water."*

"Yet, important as the proteins are in the living phenomena, **there can be no life unless there is also water.** *Thus, whether in the form of contractile proteins or functioning enzyme, living protoplasm always contains water; the unique behaviour it manifests, reflects not the behaviour of the proteins per se but that of the protein water systems.* **The question arises: In what way does water serve this critical role?** *Does it function merely as a solvent of a suitable dielectric property?"*[10] (bold added)

Almost a half century later, a team of Bioengineering from the University of Washington believe they have the answer. They came up with a new concept regarding water, the *'exclusion zone water'*, or *EZ water* (as Dr. Gerald Pollack, the head of the research team, calls it).

Not only that this *EZ water* defies many well-established principles in the fields of Physics and Chemistry (osmosis, evaporation, freezing, capillary action or Brownian motion, just to mention a few), but it comes with a new chemical formula: H_3O_2.

The new-discovered *EZ water* might explain why water is gathering only into a few wandering white clouds on a clear blue sky (even above the oceans, although it evaporates from all the Earth's surface), how do clouds made up of dense water droplets float in the sky, how plant roots are able to overcome the resistance of the soil (penetrating even the asphalt with ease, in the moment of germination), how water is rising hundreds of feet to the top of gigantic trees (against tens of atmospheres of pressure, defying Earth's gravity), or why do we sink in dry sand but not in wet sand.

---

[10] *The physical state of water in living cell and model systems*, Annals of the New York Academy of Sciences, Volume 125, October 1965, *Forms of Water in Biological Systems*, pp. 401–417, DOI: 10.1111/j.1749-6632.1965.tb45406.x

But let's see what the researchers did. Dr. Pollack's discovery can be described (in a very simplified way), as something like this: let's picture a beaker filled with water, in which the water molecules are resembled with hundreds of thousands of little tiny particles (microspheres), all mingled together.

According to standard rules of Chemistry the microspheres (or the water molecules) would be evenly suspended and distributed throughout most of the water from the beaker.

Yet, Dr. Pollack's team discovered that near the sides of the beaker there is an exclusion zone (*EZ zone*), in which the water remains clear and free of any microspheres.

The research team performed experiments on roughly a hundred hydrophilic substances (remember the Greek '*love*'), and discovered the formation of an exclusion zone of several thousand of molecules thick (in some cases, the *EZ zone* being visible with the naked eye). What intrigued the scientists was that, same as the water found in the crystals of ice, this *EZ zone* water, profoundly excludes almost everything (not just suspended particles but also the tiniest solutes).

Ok, ok, and what's the big deal? (some might say) What has to do some scientific laboratory experiment, performed on '*water loving*' substances, or this *EZ water*, with us and our bodies?

Well, scientists discovered that, unlike "pure water" (or H_2O), the water in the *EZ zone* has a net negative charge. Here, allow me to make a quick clarification and mention the fact that, contrary to the popular misconception that "*water and electricity make a dangerous pair together*", pure H_2O (such as distilled water or water condensed from the steam), does not conduct electricity and is actually an excellent insulator. However, in the real world, water almost always has some other elements dissolved in it (remember, the '*universal solvent*').

Back to Dr. Pollack's discovery, he says that "*everybody knows that the cell is negatively charged. If you insert an electrode into any of your cells, you'll measure a negative electrical potential. The textbook says that the reason for this negative electrical potential has something to do with the membrane and the ion channels in the membrane.*

Oddly, if you look at a gel that has no membrane, you record much the same potential – 100 millivolts or 150 millivolts negative. The interior of the cell is much like a gel. It's kind of surprising that something without a membrane yields the same electrical potential as the cell with a membrane. That raises the question: where does this negativity come from?

Well, I think the negativity comes from the water, because the EZ water inside the cell has a negative charge. The same is true of the gel—the EZ water in the gel confers negativity. I think the cells are negatively charged because the water inside the cell is mainly EZ water and not neutral H₂O

is mainly EZ water and not neutral H_2O", explains Dr. Pollack.[11] (bold added)

So basically, we are not just a bunch of H_2O molecules, as many believe, but rather, according to Dr. Pollacks findings, trillions of H_3O_2 cells.

Now, truth is that in the real world, on this Blue Planet (in oceans, lakes, rivers and any others flowing waters, including that 92% from our blood), there's no such thing as "pure H_2O", as found in the scientists' labs.

"The formula of water H_2O could only be a simplification, perhaps admissible in the state of steam, but certainly not in the liquid state where there are ionized molecules. Water has been proved to contain H_3O+ though in a small quantity, it also appears to contain H_5O_2+, H_7O_3+. It is now accepted that hydronium (H_3O+) is an acid since it can give up a proton to the basic hydroxyl OH- which then becomes H_2O. H_2O is thus either an acid or a base, depending upon the medium, because in giving up one proton OH- remains, and in taking a proton up there is H_3O+ (Water is therefore amphiprotic).", wrote the French scientist C. Louis Kervran in his *Biological Transmutations*.

And if we take into account the variety of ions and molecules, water represents a mixture a mixture of 18 different molecular compounds and 15 different kinds of ions, making a total of 33 different substances.[12] All of which, we are referring to as "water", yet, none of which being merely H_2O. Not to mention the fact that water is strongly influenced by temperature and pressure (for example on top of the Mount Everest, water boils at 68°C/154 °F, as opposed to 100°C/212 °F, temperature valid ONLY at sea level) and, from an accurate, scientific point of view, we're are all located on this Blue Planet at different altitudes, we have slightly different core temperatures, and so on.

But let's not digress. Let's go back to Dr. Pollack and the *EZ water* from our cells. The Bioengineering team discovered that the water found in the *EZ zone* absorbs electromagnetic energy in the ultraviolet range (with a peak of absorption at 270 nanometres). For those familiar with the electromagnetic spectrum, that's just shy of the visible range.

Moreover, when the researchers applied electromagnetic energy, they found that the *EZ water* builds and doesn't diminish. And not only that it holds energy, much like a battery, but it can deliver energy too! (you have to admit, this is pretty wild)

Dr. Polack's team propose that, since everything on this Blue Planet (and in fact, everything in the Universe) is subject to electromagnetic radiation, their findings are profound. I agree with them, and perhaps you will too, after

[11] Dr. Joseph Mercola, *The Fourth Phase of Water - What You Don't Know About Water, and Really Should*, interview with Dr. Gerard Pollack, published on August 18, 2013)
[12] K.S. Davis and J.A. Day, *Water - The Mirror of Science*, Heinemann Educational, London, 1964.

getting a little familiar with the electromagnetism (about which you'll read a lot, especially in the last chapter, and I'm sure you'll understand what's the deal with it).

Dr. Pollack even argues that this may be *"the most significant scientific discovery of this century"*, as he introduces his book, *"The Fourth Phase of Water: Beyond Solid, Liquid, and Vapor"*, published in 2013 (no affiliation or monetization whatsoever, I just found it very interesting).

"I began to think about water in the context of biology: if water inside the cell was ordered and structured and not bulk water or ordinary water as most biochemists and cell biologists think, then it is really important," says Dr. Pollack.

"The more anomalies we have, the more we begin to think that maybe there's something fundamental about water that we really don't know. *That's the core of what I'm trying to do. In our laboratory at the University of Washington, we've done many experiments over the last decade. These experiments have clearly shown the existence of this additional phase of water."* [13] (emphasis added)

Now, when it comes about the *"most significant discovery"* regarding water, let me tell you that (in my own personal opinion), many other scientific findings could compete for this title. For example, back in the 1980s, scientists from the French National Institute of Health and Medical Research (*l'Institut National de la Santé et de la Recherche Médicale* in French, shortened INSERM), came up with a concept, which, when I first heard about it, sounded like something depicted from a future sci-fi movie.

They proposed that **water has memory**! Meaning that not only it dissolves and carries around other particles and chemical elements (this thing, that water is the *'universal solvent'* can be noticed by anybody, without having too many "high academic degrees", every time we leave some dishes to soak in the sink), but it also has the ability to record, store and transmit electromagnetic information.

Moreover, the guy who came up with the "water memory" concept was a pretty "big-gun" in the medical community. Not a Nobel Prize winner, but still… His name was Dr. Jacques Benveniste, and at the time when he came up with this mind-boggling concept, he was the Director of the INSERM Research Unit 200-*Immunology of Allergy and Inflammation*.

Benveniste made a breakthrough in the medical community back in the 1970s, when he discovered the first phospholipid known to have messenger functions, the platelet-activating factor (PAF). He was the Head of the Research team in Hypersensitivity and Immediate immunopathology, of the

---

[13] Dr. Joseph Mercola, *The Fourth Phase of Water - What You Don't Know About Water, and Really Should*, interview with Dr. Gerard Pollack, published on August 18, 2013)

INSERM Unit 25-*Kidney and Immunology of Transplantation*, from 1973 until 1978, when he was appointed Director of Research. In 1979, he published a well-known paper on the structure of PAF and its relationship with histamine and became a prestigious name in Immunopathology. He was appointed Member of the INSERM Scientific Specialized Committee *Biology and General Molecular Pathology, General Immunology, Genetics, General Virology, Bacteriology, Parasitology* (1979-1982) and Member of the Scientific Council of INSERM (1983-1986). Now, I know that most of these words sound a little gibberish for a lot of readers, but if you are curious what they mean, Google is your friend.

Anyway, in my opinion, Dr. Benveniste knew what he was talking about. But let's see what he discovered, and for those who want to deepen the subject, I placed tons of footnotes (including scientific papers, newspapers and film documentaries).

Long story short, in 1983 (while he was the Director of the INSERM research unit 200-*Immunology of Allergy and Inflammation*), Dr. Benveniste received a bizarre request from one of his colleagues: to see if he can obtain some measurable effects on human cells by using some medical agents diluted through homoeopathically prepared samples.

When Benveniste received this request, he was "*one of the most classical MD, the most classical scientist and the most rationalistic person you can find*" (as he described himself) and when he first heard the word 'homeopathy', he believed that is "*a sexual disease*". [14]

Thus, he gave permission to his colleague to use the medical instruments from his laboratory, strongly convinced that there would be no measurable effects (since the main component used was only sterilized water). However, contrary to Benveniste's initial doubts, his colleague experiment succeeded.

Intrigued, Benveniste decided to study the phenomenon more closely. He asked one of his top technicians to dilute their own solutions, in exactly the same way homeopaths make their remedies, by successive dilutions in water, interspersed by vigorous shakings.

In his experiments, Dr. Benveniste used distilled water (which, is obtained by collecting into a container the steam resulted from boiling water, thus is considered by the scientists close to pure H_2O), and an antiserum used for testing people's blood for allergies (anti-immunoglobin E, or a-lgE).

[14] *Jacques Benveniste – Homeopathy*, BBC2 TV, ep. 1 of the series *Heretics*, aired on Jul 05, 1994, approx. min. 2:25 of 29:24

They mixed a small part of the antiserum (a-lgE) in some distilled water and shake vigorously the solution. The resulted solution was added to another 99 parts of distilled water, mixed again, and further added to another 99 parts of water, mixed again, added to another 99 parts, and so on.

Now, according to the well-established laws of Physics and Chemistry, when a solution is diluted by a factor of ten, after the second dilution becomes a hundred times weaker. By the sixth dilution becomes a million times weaker, by the ninth dilution becomes a billionth times weaker, and so on. Statistically speaking, according to the Avogadro's constant, after 23 dilutions there should be no molecule of the initial solution left in the final resulted solution.

But let's understand what scientists did. For that, let's take a glass filled with water and a sugar cube. Ok, the researchers used different ratios of some 'water-loving' solution and 'pure H_2O', but in order to understand what they did, we will go with a sugar cube and couple of glasses of water.

Now, we drop the sugar cube into the cup and we mix the water until the sugar if completely dissolved. If we taste the water, we'll notice that it's a little sweeter than the original, right?

Now let's take a second cup, identical in size as the first one, fill it with regular water, and add to it a spoon from the first cup (that contains the sweet water, or the mother-tincture). After we mix the water from the second cup and taste it, we'll notice that is not as sweet as the water from the first cup (makes sense, right?).

Now we take a third cup, same size, fill it again with water, and add to it a spoon of the water that we have in the second cup. According to the scientific terminology, we are now at the third dilution, and the initial mother-tincture (the water from the first cup, in which we dissolved the sugar cube) became a thousand times weaker.

In fact, you can even taste the water from the first cup and compare it with the taste of the water from the third cup. Maybe (just maybe), only if you would give someone else, who has no clue of your little scientific experiment, to taste the water from the third cup first and after that the sweet water from the first cup (I strongly emphasise "maybe") he could spot some tint of sweet in the water. If he tastes the mother-tincture first, and after that the water from the third cup, he wouldn't spot nothing. He would say is just plain water.

Now, if we take one spoon from the third cup, we add it to a brand-new glass of water and we mix it, we getting the fourth dilution. Take another spoon and another cup full of water (fifth dilution), and, I hope you see where I'm going, we continue the procedure up to 23 times.

In the last cup, the initial mother-tincture would be a hundred trillion of billions weaker (or 10^{23}, for our mathematician's friends). That's a pretty huge number, and in fact, you can even taste the water from the 23rd cup, see if you feel any sweet taste.

In simple terms, this are the "highly diluted" solutions used by the researchers, and this is the basis for homeopathy. However, since it defies the current scientific understanding, it's not so easily to accept by many people (including scientists).

Now, let's see what Dr. Benveniste's team discovered. Strangely, as the they were keep diluting the mother-tincture (containing the a-lgE), when particular blood cells were exposed to the highest diluted solution, they were reading results as if the cells were exposed to the to the initial concentration of antiserum alg-E.

This fact got Dr. Benveniste intrigued, and, determined to find an explanation for the phenomenon, he diluted the antiserum even 120 times. That means a dilution of 1 part to 10^{120} parts of distilled water, five times more than the limit set by the Avogadro's constant. Still, when the resulted highly-diluted solution was exposed to the blood cells, **the cells reacted as they were in the presence of the original antiserum** (admit it, sounds pretty wild).

It was as, somehow, the water molecules "retained the memory" of the antibodies they had been previously in contact with, and carried that biological effect even when the antibodies were no longer present.

The only rational explanation that Dr. Benveniste could find was that water was, somehow, capable to "memorize" the molecules it entered contact with at the beginning of the dilution, and billions of billions of billions of dilutions after, it still "knew" that it had "seen" that molecules.

Excited by this new discovery regarding water, Dr. Benveniste sent his work to *Nature*, one of the world's leading scientific journals. The *Nature*'s editor sent the paper to referees, which all said that, although the scientific work is very impressive, they do not believe a word in it. It defies all the conventional understanding of science.

However, *Nature* agreed to publish Benveniste's paper, with two unusual conditions: first, Prof. Benveniste had to obtain prior confirmation of his results from other laboratories, and, secondly, a team of experts selected by *Nature* to be allowed to investigate his laboratory, following publication.

Benveniste sent his researches to four other laboratories (from Canada, France, Israel and Italy), which all successfully replicated and confirmed his experiments, and, after a lengthy review process, *Nature* published Prof. Benveniste's paper, on June 30, 1988.[15]

---

[15] E. Davenas, F. Beauvais, J. Amara, M. Oberbaum, B. Robinzon, A. Miadonnai, A. Tedeschi, B.

Benveniste's "water memory" became a media sensation all over the world, giving rise to polemics in the entire mass-media and in the medical community.

Soon after the publication of Benveniste's paper, *Nature* sent his own committee of investigators to the INSERM. However, instead of sending some medical authorities in the fields of Molecular Biology, Immunology or Immunopathology (this was, basically, the nature of Dr. Benveniste's studies), *Nature*'s team of investigators was composed of Walter Stewart (a chemist and freelance debunker), James Randi (magician and paranormal researcher) and John Maddox, *Nature*'s editor (who manifested a high note of scepticism even when Dr. Benveniste's original paper was published).

They spent a week verifying Prof. Benveniste's research, questioned his team, investigated the notebooks from earlier experiments, took pictures, and even set up video cameras (looking for some "hidden tricks"), before conducting their own experiments. They performed only one experiment and concluded that *Benveniste's results are being widely interpreted as support for homeopathic medicine"* and that *"the phenomenon described is not reproducible."* [16]

This, despite the fact that Walter Stewart declared that *"the uniformity of some test results was disturbing"*, while James Randi stated that he doubted that there had been any *"conscious fraud"*.

As a response to *Nature*'s committee of "experts" in Immunology and Immunopathology – in the same issue (no. 334, 28 July 1988, pp. 287–290), and in a subsequent commentary –, Prof. Benveniste accused *Nature* team's with *"mockery of scientific inquiry"*.

He complained that the investigating team created an atmosphere of *"constant suspicion"*, pointed that they arrived without a prior plan, and one week of their work *"would blot out five years of our work and that of five other laboratories"*. He charged the team of non-biologists with *"amateurism"*, who failed to *"get to grips with our biological system"*, arguing that such *"Salem witch-hunts or McCarthy-like prosecutions will kill science."*

"Clearly, the short sightedness of two high priests of orthodox science [John Maddox and Walter Stewart] *and a prestidigitator* [Randi] *have delayed the advance in Chemistry and Biology by ten years"*, complained Benveniste.

Benveniste's discovery turned into "Benveniste affair". By suggesting that *"water retains the memory of molecules it once contained"*, Prof. Benveniste became both target and victim of orthodox science and medicine.

Pomeranz, P. Fortner, P. Belon, J. Sainte-Laudy, B. Poitevin & J. Benveniste, *Human basophil degranulation triggered by very dilute antiserum against IgE*, Nature 333, 816–818 (30 June 1988), doi:10.1038/333816a0

[16] John Maddox, James Randi & Walter W. Stewart, *"High-dilution" experiments a delusion*, Nature 334, 287–290 (28 July 1988), doi:10.1038/334287a0

* * * * * *

"I constantly ask myself 'What did I do wrong?'...Maybe I should have thrown the data's away...If I am right or I am wrong that's not the problem. The problem is to change the system. As strange as it might sound, science has become unfriendly to new ideas.
If we can be, as scientists, stamped as heretics is because there is a dogma. And the fact that all dogmas have been crushed in the past by new ideas is not a lesson for these people."
Prof. Dr. Jacques Benveniste (1935 – 2004)

* * * * * *

Shortly after *Nature*'s evaluation, another world-renowned biostatistician and epidemiologist (Prof. Dr. Alfred Spira, the then Director of INSERM research unit 292-*Public Health, Epidemiology and Human Reproduction*), set up a blind test of Benveniste's discredited experiments.

"I was really upset and surprised after the publication of Benveniste's paper in Nature, when I read the evaluation which was made by the editor of the journal, a magician and a journalist...It could be dangerous for scientists to be evaluated in such a way", declared Dr. Spira in an interview for BBC2 TV.[17]

So, Prof. Spira's team diluted their own set of allergens to the point that they would be only water, according to the same homeopathic techniques used by Prof. Benveniste. They secretly relabelled the test tubes (using a code known only to them), they included a set of fake tubes containing nothing but water, and they sent all the samples to Prof. Benveniste's laboratory, to see if his team can spot the real dilutions from the fake ones. Against Dr. Spira's expectations, the results came up the same as Benveniste's initial experiments.

Recalling the situation, Dr. Spira declared that he was *"very surprised"*. *"We found the same results as Jacques Benveniste published in Nature. Everything was blind and there was absolutely no possibility of cheating or fraud in interpreting the data."*[18]

Weirdly, even Dr. Spira's blind experiment was disregarded by the medical community.

In July 1989, one year after *Nature* published its conclusions, INSERM placed Prof. Benveniste on probation, following a routine evaluation of his laboratory. Although they found that the activities were overall exemplary, they expressed severe discomfort with Prof. Benveniste's high dilution studies.

---

[17] *Jacques Benveniste – Homeopathy*, BBC2 TV, ep. 1 of the series *Heretics*, aired on Jul 05, 1994, approx. min. 16:20 of 29:24
[18] Ibid. approx. min. 17:20 of 29.24

Four years later, things got even worse. In October 1993, Prof. Benveniste was evicted from the INSERM unit 200, and transferred from his laboratories (spanning multiple floors, on an area of 450m²/c. 4,850 sq. ft.), into an annex of 100 m² (about 1,070 sq. ft.).

* * * * * *

"It is as if they were afraid to discover something that they didn't like. It's reasonable that people should be sceptical, and should demand good proof, but what I think is not reasonable, is to refuse any proof."
Dr. Michel Schiff (1933 – 2004)

* * * * * *

However, Prof. Benveniste didn't lose his faith. He considered this event a *"nice change of atmosphere"*, in an environment with *"strong interactions between analysts, due to crowding"*.[19]

Strongly convinced of the accuracy of his scientific studies, he founded the *Jacques Benveniste Association for Research*, led by a scientific committee composed of multi-disciplinary scientists (researchers in Biology, theoretical Physics, doctors and epistemologists, from several countries, including France, Italy, Russia and the USA).

Still, when INSERM announced that is planning to shut down his immunopharmacology unit, Prof. Benveniste had to find new ways to figure out the "mysteries of water".

He set up his own research company, and bought a set of standard laboratory apparatus, in order to continue his researches by testing new drugs on killed rat's hearts. He wanted to find if a drug, homoeopathically diluted to the point that it was only water, could behave like the original drug.

After years of research and hundreds of experiments, Prof. Benveniste managed to successful obtain a biological activity with very high dilutions. In an interview for BBC2 TV (aired in 1994), Prof. Benveniste declared that *"we have hundreds of experiments that are clearly demonstrating the fact that we can get biological activity, very successfully, with very high dilutions. It is a major pharmacological effect, obtained with nothing else than water in a dilution. The next obvious question is how water can do it. What are the physical mechanisms behind this possibility, the capability of water to transfer a biological information?"*[20] (emphasis added)

---

[19] *"On a retrouvé la mémoire de l'eau"* (*"We rediscovered the memory of water"*), Doc En Stock, France, aired on France 5, 2014, approx. min. 05:05 of 51:50
[20] *Jacques Benveniste – Homeopathy*, BBC2 TV, ep. 1 of the series *Heretics*, aired on Jul 05, 1994, approx. min. 19:50 of 29:24

Determined to crack the water's "secret code", Dr. Benveniste placed some highly dilute drug solutions into a powerful magnetic coil to erase any possible electromagnetic information. When he retested the solution, it proved to have no effect.

This brought Prof. Benveniste to the conclusion that water has something like an electromagnetic memory system. Pursuing this hypothesis, he placed a test tube containing highly diluted solution of a toxin on top of a coil, amplified its electromagnetic signal, and, in about the same way as a telephone receiver transmits the human voice, the signal was transmitted to another coil, on top of which was placed another container, containing only saline water.

After the second tube (containing only saline water) "charged" with the electromagnetic signal emitted by the mother-tincture, Benveniste injected the saline solution into a rat's heart. The heart went into a complete arrhythmia, reacting as it was injected with the toxic compound, despite the fact that the saline water from the second container never came in direct physical contact with any molecule of the mother-tincture. This brought Benveniste to the conclusion that water is a *"liquid magnetic tape"*.

★ ★ ★ ★ ★ ★

"For the first time in the history of mankind we can transfer a biological information to a magnetic kind of liquid tape, which is water."
Prof. Jacques Benveniste (1935 – 2004)

★ ★ ★ ★ ★ ★

While Dr. Benveniste was performing these experiments, scientists from all over the world were trying to replicate his findings.

In the 1990s, a consortium of four independent research laboratories from France, Italy, Belgium, and Holland used a refinement of Prof. Benveniste's original experiment. They tried to reproduce the results, leaving no room for fraud or wishful thinking, by comparing the inhibition of basophil a-lgE induced degranulation with "ghost" dilutions of histamine, against control solutions of pure water.

To make sure that no bias was introduced into the experiment the researchers from all four laboratories were "blinded" to the contents of their test solutions. This means they didn't know whether the solutions they were adding to the basophil-algE reaction contained "ghost" amounts of histamine, or just pure water. To make the experiment as accurate as possible, both the "ghost" histamine solutions and the controls were prepared in three other different laboratories, that had nothing further to do with the trial.

Finally, the whole experiment was coordinated by an independent researcher who was not involved in any of the testing or analysis of the data from the experiment, and who coded all the solutions and collated the data.

Three out of four laboratories involved in the trial reported a "statistically significant result", while the fourth lab gave a result that was "almost significant", bringing the final conclusion of the four independent laboratories as positive.

Prof. Benveniste didn't seem too impressed by their study. He declared for the British newspaper *The Guardian* that *"they've arrived at precisely where we started 12 years ago!"*[21]

In 1999, another large pan-European research team, led by Prof. Madeleine Ennis of Queen's University of Belfast, tried to prove that Prof. Benveniste is wrong. Yet, they came out with controversially results, and had to admit that Prof. Benveniste might have been right all along.[22]

Another experiment, performed by theoretical physicist Lynn Trainor of the University of Toronto, showed that after the mother-tincture had been diluted 37 times, it was more than twice as effective as a solution that had been diluted thrice.[23]

Intrigued by Prof. Benveniste's findings, even the U.S. Defence Advanced Research Projects Agency (DARPA) became interested in his studies about water's memory. They designated Dr. Wayne B. Jonas (the then Director of the U.S. National Centre for Complementary and Alternative Medicine) to assemble a multidisciplinary team and investigate the phenomenon. The team included Prof. Benveniste (as a consultant), a haematologist, an engineer, a statistician, a neuroscientist, a conflict management expert and a sceptic. Funded by the U.S. Department of Defence, Dr. Jonas' team tried to replicate Benveniste's results, however, by using the same experimental devices and setup as in the original experiments, they failed to find any effect.

They noted several results only when a particular researcher from Benveniste's team was running the equipment (and you will understand why in the next chapter). Even Prof. Benveniste admitted that he noticed himself that *"certain individuals consistently get digital effects and other individuals get no effects or block those effects"*. [24]

---

[21] Lionel Milgrom, *Thanks for the memory*, The Guardian, March 14, 2001

[22] Belon, P., Cumps, J., Ennis, M. et al. Inflamm. res. (1999) 48(Suppl 1): 17. doi: 10.1007/s000110050376

[23] Callum Coats, *Living Energies: Viktor Schauberger's brilliant work with natural energies explained*, Gill & MacMillan, 2001, p. 120

[24] Wayne B. Jonas et al., *Can specific biological signals be digitized?*, FASEB Journal, January 2006, vol. 20, no. 1 23-28, doi:10.1096/fj.05-3815hyp

The DARPA conclusion was that water, under the influence of digital signals recorded on a computer disc, is not producing any specific biological effects.

However, Prof. Benveniste went even further with his researches. He equipped his laboratory with a robot, to carry out the experiments with no need for human intervention. He improved the techniques of recording the signals and reproduced more than a thousand times the effects of high dilution.

He even played the signals back to cells in the absence of the molecules themselves. Not only that he managed to reproduce their biochemical effect, but he even triggered a defence response in neutrophils (a type of white blood cell that help the body fight infections and heal injuries).

His explanation for these strange results was that *"biomolecules communicate with their receptor molecules by sending out low-frequency electromagnetic signals, which the receptors pick up like radios tuned to a specific wavelength"*. [25]

* * * * * *

"It was very, very clear that water was in fact a liquid magnetic tape. And if water was doing this job in our tests is because it was doing this job in Nature, in your own body, between your own cells, or my cells, or my molecules...We might have uncovered the language of molecules, which is a kind of a step forward in science."
Prof. Dr. Jacques Benveniste (1935 – 2004)

* * * * * *

Regarding water properties, things didn't stop here in the scientific community. Without being related with Dr. Benveniste's discoveries, engineers and quantum physicians discovered that water has "memory cells", and inside every molecule of water exist 440,000 information panels, each of which responsible for its own type of interaction with the environment.

According to Prof. Rustum Roy (1924-2010), world-known leader in materials research and member of U.S. National Academy of Engineering, water *"may be the single most malleable computer. Is like a computer memory. Is the memory of information. We must know how it is arranged. It's like the alphabet, you don't know a word, you don't know a letter, you don't know a sentence. So, the molecular structure is the alphabet of water. And you must make a sentence out of water and change the sentence."* [26]

[25] Y. Thomas, M. Schiff, L. Belkadi, P. Jurgens, L. Kahhak, J. Benveniste, *Activation of human neutrophils by electronically transmitted phorbol-myristate acetate.*, Medical Hypotheses, January 2000, Vol. 54, Issue 1, Pages 33–39, DOI: http://dx.doi.org/10.1054/mehy.1999.0891
[26] Russian documentary *"Вода" (Water)*, written by Saida Medvedeva and Sergey Shumakov, directed by Julia Perkul and Anastasiya Popova, released in Russia and USA in 2008, approx. min 09:45 of 1:23:16

Yet, while engineers know for sure that water has information panels, and even that salt water burns, with flames, when certain electric voltage is applied (a thing that shouldn't surprise us, since oxygen, besides its old name of *'vital air'* was also known as the *'fire air'*), the fact that water has "memory" remains a cool thing.

Although there are still many sceptics out there, and Dr. Benveniste's discoveries are regarded by the mainstream scientific community as a fraud, more than two decades after Prof. Benveniste's came up with the "water memory" designation, another well-renowned name in the medical community continued Benveniste's researches. This time, the joint recipient of the 2008 Nobel Prize in Physiology or Medicine (for his part in establishing that the human immunodeficiency virus causes AIDS), Prof. Dr. Luc Antoine Montagnier.

Not only that Prof. Montagnier is a world-known famous virologist, but he holds many respectable positions in the academic community: he is a member of the France *Académie Nationale de Médecine* (National Academy of Medicine), co-founder of the World Foundation for AIDS Research and Prevention, co-director of the Program for International Viral Collaboration, Founder and former president of the Houston-based World Foundation for Medical Research and Prevention. He received over 20 major awards: the France *Ordre national du Mérite* (National Order of Merit) in rank of Commander in 1986, the *Ordre national de la Légion d'honneur* (National Order of the Legion of Honour), the highest French order of merit (in rank of Knight in 1984, Officer in 1990, Commander in 1993, and Grand Officer in 2009), the King Faisal Foundation International Prize (also known as the Arab Nobel Prize) in 1993, among many others.

"I always searched for the unusual. It is hard for me to work on an established theory. I prefer to innovate", declared Prof. Montagnier in 2014, in an interview for the public French television France5, in a documentary film, *On a retrouvé la mémoire de l'eau (We rediscovered the memory of water)*.[27]

Driven by curiosity, he applied Prof. Benveniste's technologies on his own research, on blood plasma of people infected with HIV. Contrary to his initial expectations, he detected from the first experiments that water was emitting electromagnetic signals.

---

[27] *"On a retrouvé la mémoire de l'eau"* (*"We rediscovered the memory of water"*), Doc En Stock, France, aired on France 5, 2014, approx. min. 01:45 of. 51:50

Fascinated by the phenomenon, Prof. Montagnier resumed Dr. Benveniste's work, and started his own researches. After years of studies, he published two controversial papers[28,29], in which concluded that *"diluted DNA from pathogenic bacterial and viral species is able to emit specific radio waves"*, and that *"these radio waves [are] associated with 'nanostructures' in the solution that might be able to recreate the pathogen"*.

As in the case of his predecessor, Prof. Montagnier discoveries are defying the conventional scientific understanding. According to an article published in the *New Scientist*, if Prof. Montagnier conclusions are true, this *"would be the most significant experiment performed in the past 90 years, demanding re-evaluation of the whole conceptual framework of modern chemistry."*[30]

* * * * * *

"These facts are very hard to admit for a certain number of our colleague's, including Nobel laureates, who are discussing very fiercely these ideas, but these are facts, facts established through reproducible scientific experiments"
Prof. Dr. Luc Montagnier (Nobel Prize in Physiology or Medicine, 2008)

* * * * * *

During an experiment recorded by the France5, Dr. Montagnier successfully proved that water has "memory" and "remembers" the electromagnetic signature of other substances previously dissolved in it.

His team dissolved one volume of DNA molecules from an HIV infected patient into nine volumes of sterile water. Now, remember the cup of water and the sugar cube from Benveniste's example? In Prof. Montagnier case, the "sugar cube" consisted of 2 nano-grams (2×10^{-9}) of DNA, an astronomically tiny quantity.

The first dilution was vigorously shacked in a vortex mixer for 15 seconds, then added to another nine volumes of sterile water. Therefore, resulted the second dilution (D2). This was again added to another nine volumes of sterile water, resulting D3, and so on, the procedure was sequentially repeated up to the 10th dilution.

---

[28] Montagnier, L., Aïssa, J., Ferris, S. et al., *Electromagnetic signals are produced by aqueous nanostructures derived from bacterial DNA sequence*, Interdiscip Sci Comput Life Sci, June 2009, Volume 1, Issue 2, pp 81. doi: 10.1007/s12539-009-0036-7

[29] Montagnier, L., Aïssa, J., Lavallée, C. et al., *Electromagnetic detection of HIV DNA in the blood of AIDS patients treated by antiretroviral therapy*, Interdiscip Sci Comput Life Sci, December 2009, Volume 1, Issue 4, pp 245. doi: 10.1007/s12539-009-0059-0

[30] Andy Coghlan, *Scorn over claim of teleported DNA*, New Scientist 12 January 2011, issue 2795

Theoretically, if they would have been carried out the procedure up to 23 times, it would have been the equivalent of diluting one drop of the original DNA into the Atlantic Ocean. Even so, from the biological point of view, even at the 10th dilution, there shouldn't be not even a single molecule of DNA from the initial mother-tincture present in the final dilution.

To avoid the risk of fraud, or influence on the experiment results, the test-tubes were encoded, following a double-blind procedure. On one hand, a member of the TV crew labelled the test-tubes (marking with random numbers each label), making thus impossible to know which of the tubes correspond to different dilutions. For example, let's say that a particular tube contained the sixth dilution (D6). The TV member crew mark it with D2, or whatever, D9.

Then he added ten more test tubes, containing only sterile water, and sent all 20 tubes (the ones containing the dilutions D1-D10, plus the ten "fake" test-tubes) to another to another laboratory, to Dr. Jamal Aissa (one of Benveniste's old collaborators, who joined Dr. Montaginer in deciphering "water's memory").

Dr. Aissa placed the tubes on a special sensor, similar to a microphone, and recorded the electromagnetic signal generated by each tube. The signals were digitalized and stored as a computer file, on a hard drive.

After he analysed the recordings, Dr. Aissa successfully identified the tubes containing the water "charged" from the DNA molecules, despite the fact that there were 10 "fake" tubes involved in the experiment (containing nothing but water), while the rest of D10 solutions were diluted to such a high degree that not even a single DNA molecule should have remained in the water.

If we really think about it, only at this point, when Prof. Montagnier's team spotted the tubes that were emitting particular electromagnetic signals, we realize that Prof. Benveniste was right all along. Water retained the "memory" of the original DNA traces.

Yet, Prof. Montagnier went even further. The electromagnetic signals were sent in Italy (to the University of Sannio, Benevento, located 1,500 km/930 miles away), through the internet, as email attachment.

At the Italian University, famous for the quality of its laboratories specialized in Molecular Biology, the experiment was carried out the other way around, by Prof. Dr. Giuseppe Vitiello, Ph.D. (another world leading authority in the field of Theoretical Physics). In fact, he is world-renowned for his research activity in quantum field theory, gauge theories, non-linear dynamical systems, biological systems and brain physics, but, as I mentioned in the preface, we can't say that water belongs only to one particular field of research (Biochemistry, Genetics, Astronomy, Meteorology, or whatever).

Instead, IT manifests its presence in ALL fields of Science, and we, as humans, we discover new things about IT every day, from different perspectives. On our Blue Planet, and in the entire Universe, Water remains Water, and slowly, IT uncovers its mysteries.

In Italy, Prof. Vitiello downloaded the e-mail from France (containing the recording of the electromagnetic signal) and "played the sound" to a single isolated tube, containing only purified water. After about an hour, during whih the water "listened" the recordings from France, Dr. Vitiello applied on the sterile water the polymerase chain reaction technique (PCR), a technique used in many fields of science, including molecular biology and forensic science, for the identification of criminals (this one you should really Google it, cause it's pretty cool). Basically, the technique means that a single copy (or a few copies) of a segment of DNA is amplified, generating thousands to millions of copies that of that particular DNA sequence (it's pretty wild what scientists can do these days).

Out of pure water, Dr. Vitiello successfully reconstructed the original DNA sequence from France, although that there were no physical DNA molecules present and the water from Italy never came into contact with the original mother-tincture located in Paris, 1,500 km away.

Thus, is an established scientific fact (despite many unbelievers) that water is capable of recording, memorize, and transmit (in the form of electromagnetic signals) the information of other molecules previously dissolved in it. This means that if somebody would pour a bottle of Coke into a mountain river, thousands of miles away, where the water from the river flows into a sea, the water from sea water will "know" that it "tasted" some "sweet stuff". Feel free to replace the bottle of coke with whatever "water-loving" substance, including poisons and why-not.

This fact *"makes a lot of people to grind their teeth, because is not so easy to explain"* says Prof. Montagnier.[31]

"Of course, there are many things to be explained, it is not understood completely. Very often science does not give answers but opens questions. So, we now have more questions than before, just because it works"[32], declared Prof. Giuseppe Vitiello for the France television.

---

[31] "On a retrouvé la mémoire de l'eau" ("We rediscovered the memory of water"), Doc En Stock, France, aired on France 5, 2014, approx. min. 25:45 of. 51:50
[32] ibid. min. 25:55

Although Prof. Montagnier and Prof. Vitiello published several scientific papers regarding DNA transduction[33],[34], as in Prof. Benveniste's case, the results raised big controversies in the scientific community and causing fierce polemics between the orthodox medical system (including Montagnier's fellow Nobel Prize winners) and homeopaths, eager for greater credibility.

On 28 June, 2010, Prof. Montagnier held a speech at the Lindau Nobel Laureate Meeting, in Germany, where, according to the media[35] *"60 Nobel prize winners had gathered, along with 700 other scientists, to discuss the latest breakthroughs in medicine, chemistry and physics"*. The article states that Prof. Montagnier *"stunned his colleagues...when he presented a new method for detecting viral infections that bore close parallels to the basic tenets of homeopathy"*.

However, Prof. Montagnier never mentioned homeopathy in his studies. Moreover, in an interview for Canada's CBC *Marketplace* program, he clearly stated that he *"cannot extrapolate* [his research] *to the products used in homeopathy"*.[36]

* * * * * *

"It's not pseudoscience. It's not quackery.
These are real phenomena which deserve further study."
Prof. Luc Montagnier (Nobel Prize in Physiology or Medicine, 2008)

* * * * * *

On the other hand, in the homeopaths' world, Montagnier's findings caused a very big excitement. *"Montagnier's work gave homeopathy a true scientific ethos"*, declared Cristal Sumner, of the British Homeopathic Association.

Later in the same year, *Science* magazine, published an interview with Prof. Montagnier, in an article titled *French Nobelist Escapes "Intellectual Terror" to Pursue Radical Ideas in China*.[37]

During the interview, Prof. Montagnier declared that not only the DNA from patients infected with HIV produces structural changes in water, but he also detected signals coming from bacterial DNA in the plasma of many patients with autism, Alzheimer, Parkinson's disease, and multiple sclerosis.

[33] Invited talk at the DICE2010 Conference, Castglioncello, Italy, September 2010, Cornell University Library DOI: 10.1088/1742-6596/306/1/012007, https://arxiv.org/abs/1012.5166
[34] Published in 2015 in Journal of Electromagnetic Biology and Medicine, Cornell University Library DOI: 10.3109/15368378.2015.1036072, https://arxiv.org/abs/1501.01620
[35] *Nobel laureate gives homeopathy a boost*, The Australian 5 July 2010 http://www.theaustralian.com.au/
[36] *Cure Or Con?*, CBC Marketplace, archived from the original on 13 April 2014 (approx. 17:00 of 22:29). http://www.cbc.ca/marketplace/episodes/2011-episodes/cure-or-con
[37] Martin Enserink, *French Nobelist Escapes "Intellectual Terror" to Pursue Radical Ideas in China*, Science 24 Dec 2010, Vol. 330, Issue 6012, pp. 1732, DOI: 10.1126/science.330.6012.1732

These signals persist at very high dilutions and lead to measurable resonant electromagnetic signals.

He hopes that in the future (I honestly hope too), the medical system will use these findings for both, diagnostic and treatment. That's because they discovered another thing: electromagnetic waves, at particular frequencies, can "kill" the waves produced by bacterial DNA. In other words, this means that any disease would be cured with "simple" water that had "listened" some electromagnetic signals (bye-bye pharmaceutical industry).

Unfortunately, because of the French retirement law, Prof. Montagnier was unable to continue his studies in a public institution. Also, because of the controversial nature of the researches, his applications for funding had been turned down, so the long-time researcher at the Pasteur Institute in Paris had to leave his home country, to continue his work in Shanghai, China.

"I have been offered a professorship and a new institute, which will bear my name, to work on a new scientific movement at the crossroads of physics, biology, and medicine. The main topic will be this phenomenon of electromagnetic waves produced by DNA in water. We will study both the theoretical basis and the possible applications in medicine".

Sadly, as opposed to the Western system of Science, it seems that the Chinese are more open-minded to this kind of research. It's not my own personal opinion, but Prof. Montagnier's: *"I have visited Jiao Tong University several times, and they are quite open-minded",* declared Prof. Luc Montagnier for the *Science* magazine.[38]

Yet, how this information, that water has memory, and it's able to able to record, store and transmit electromagnetic information, can help us improve our lives? In order to understand this, we have to make a little trip into the unseen world of forces and energies, and from there, back into our bodies. I promise it will be captivating.

[38] Ibid.

CHAPTER 3. THE HEALING POWERS OF WATER

✶✶✶✶✶✶

"If you want to find the secrets of the universe, think in terms of energy, frequency and vibration."
Nikola Tesla (1856 – 1943)

✶✶✶✶✶✶

Before we enter the "world of magic" (the unseen world of forces and energies), I have to mention a few things. First of all, FORCES AND ENERGIES EXIST! Regardless that we're talking about the ones encountered in the ancient spiritual texts and rituals, or the ones proposed by the scientists, they are all around us and are influencing our lives in ways beyond many people's imagination.

The ones encountered in the spiritual beliefs are visible all around us, in plain sight, whenever we find ourselves in a positive or negative situation, or when we experience some positive/negative thoughts, feelings or attitudes. Now, as far as regarding "positive" and "negative", as many people, as many definitions and opinions.

As far as those encountered in science, the story tells that not even 300 years ago, Sir Isaac Newton saw an apple falling down from a tree. He proposed that the same force that pulls apples to the ground is the same force that keeps the Moon in an orbit around the Earth, and he termed it "gravity". If he would have named it, say, "cup-cake", we'd all be learning in the Physics class that "cup-cake", instead of "gravity", is responsible for breaking the coffee cup when falling off the desk (because we didn't pay attention at how close to the edge of the desk we left it). It's just a word, but we experience its effects every second of every day.

Newton is credited today for making the first step in unifying the Heavens and the Earth, because he proposed that the force that pulls apples to the ground is the same force that keeps the Moon in an orbit around the Earth. His proposal made sense, since at that time, the general belief was that the Earth was the centre of the Universe, and the cosmological model was that of Ptolemy's (in which the Sun, Moon, stars and all the planets, all are circling the Earth).

48

Yet, how gravity works remained a mystery for almost 250 years, even for mathematicians and theoretical physicists. It was only in the early 20th century when Newton's law of universal gravitation got superseded by Albert Einstein's theory of general relativity.

What Einstein basically did was that he connected the three dimensions of the space with that of the time, and realized that massive objects are causing a distortion in the structure of space-time. Thus, the current scientific explanation is that gravity moves through space as much as the same way that a pebble dropped into a pond makes ripples that travel across the surface of the water.

By the way, Einstein's discovery came about 50 years after James Clark Maxwell made (in 1865), the second "Great Unification" in Physics, when he realized that electricity, magnetism and light are different manifestations of the same phenomenon.

Since then, scientists discovered in the past century two more forces. By probing the structure of the atom, they termed the "strong force" as the force responsible for binding the fundamental particles of matter. And another force, that acts between subatomic particles and is responsible for the mechanism that causes some forms of radioactive decay, is known as the "weak force".

Truth is that when we are referring to forces or energies, we cannot actually see the force or the energy itself. All that we can perceive is the outward manifestation of the forces and energies. Their true origin, their intrinsic power, size, frequency, or vibrational state are lying beyond our physical senses.

★ ★ ★ ★ ★ ★

"Scientific research is based on the idea that everything that takes place is determined by laws of nature, and therefore this holds for the actions of people. For this reason, a research scientist will hardly be inclined to believe that events could be influenced by a prayer, i.e., by a wish addressed to a supernatural being...
But, on the other hand, everyone who is seriously involved in the pursuit of science becomes convinced that a spirit is manifest in the laws of the Universe - a spirit vastly superior to that of man, and one in the face of which we with our modest powers must feel humble."
Albert Einstein (1879 – 1955)

★ ★ ★ ★ ★ ★

Although invisible to our physical senses, forces and energies are as real as the material world we see around us, and, most of the time, they come in pairs. You can call them electricity and magnetism, heat and cold, gravitation and levitation, pressure and suction, centrifugal and centripetal movements, implosion and explosion, and so on. In the Asiatic traditions we encounter the *Yin and Yang*, while the ancient Greek philosopher Empedocles proposed that everything is under the influence of two supreme forces, *Philia* (i.e. love or attraction) and *Neikos* (i.e. strife or repulsion).

Still, the true source of these forces and energies, their true power and size, lies beyond our physical senses.

Newton didn't actually see the gravity; he only saw an apple falling down from a tree. Even ourselves, in our daily life, when we turn on the light in our room, we cannot actually see the electricity, we can only see the light coming out from the light bulb. When we are talking on the phone, listen the radio while we're driving, watching TV, browsing the internet, heating food in the microwave (and many, other countless examples), we cannot see the electromagnetic fields, although we know they are there.

Now, let's see how water can help us change our lives by understanding first the electromagnetism. This force is something that surrounds us, wherever we go, every second of every hour of every day. It is all around us, and even inside us, ALL THE TIME!

Electromagnetic waves are produced by the vibration of the charged particles and have electric and magnetic properties. They are similar to ocean waves in that both are energy waves (transmit energy), but unlike ocean waves, the electromagnetic waves can travel through the vacuum of space.

Same as water, electromagnetism is odourless, tasteless, manifests its presence all around our Blue Planet, and is generated even inside our bodies (Yes, our bodies produces water, as the end-product of the oxidation of energy-containing molecules; this water is known as metabolic water and represents about 8-10% of the water our bodies use every day).

While many doctors and academicians are still puzzled by Prof. Dr. Montagnier findings, it is a well-established fact that water interacts with the electromagnetic fields. This can be easily observed by every one of us. For example, let's turn on the faucet from the kitchen sink, or fill a container with water and drill a small hole at the bottom of the container. We'll see that water is flowing straight down, at a slow and steady speed. Now, if we take a plastic object (a pen, a comb, a straw, a PVC pipe or a plastic ruler), which we rub it to a dry towel (a fleece blanket, or even on our dry hair), in order to build up some static electricity, we'll notice that when the electrically charged object is placed next to the water flow, the water stream will bend towards the object.

No matter where we are, at home or at work, on the seashore or on the top of a mountain, we're bathing into an invisible ocean of electromagnetic waves. Our Earth has its own magnetic field, which causes a compass needle to orient in a North-South direction and is used by birds and fish for navigation. We have local build-ups of electric charges in the atmosphere, associated with thunderstorms. We have visible light waves striking our eyes, radio waves transmitting information all over the globe, microwaves carrying cell phone calls and text messages, waves from WiFi and GPS units, and so on.

However, let's suppose we place ourselves in the most shielded room on this Earth, we still can't escape from electromagnetism. That's because it is produced in our bodies, as a result of the reactions that occur as part of the normal bodily functions. Our nerves relay signals by transmitting electrical impulses, and most biochemical reactions, from digestion to brain activities, go along with the rearrangement of charged particles. Electricity and magnetism everywhere we look, inside and outside.

In fact, scientists even acknowledged this thing, and argued in a study published in 2017 that *"all biological systems on Earth are exposed to an external and internal environment of fluctuating invisible magnetic fields of a wide range of frequencies. These fields can affect virtually every cell and circuit to a greater or lesser degree."*[39]

Now, let's get back to water…

In the past decades, scientists went even deeper in studying how water interacts with the electromagnetic forces. In the 1990s, Dr. Lee Lorenzen was one of the first researchers who discovered that the water molecules are not coming as individual molecules (it's not just the simple well-known H_2O designation, where one atom of oxygen is connected with two atoms of hydrogen through covalent bonds, sharing electron pairs), instead they are gathered in clusters.

Lorenzen came up with this conclusion after his wife, Penny, was diagnosed with chronic fatigue-induced myalgia and multiple viral infections. She tried different forms of medication, vitamins, herbs, acupuncture, and chiropractic treatments, all with no results. As a final alternative, Dr. Lorenzen decided to take her in Japan, to the healing springs of Kirumisu, outside of Kyoto, and they noticed an improvement in Penny's health condition.

[39] McCraty, R.; Atkinson, M.; Stolc, V.; Alabdulgader, A.A.; Vainoras, A.; Ragulskis, M. *Synchronization of Human Autonomic Nervous System Rhythms with Geomagnetic Activity in Human Subjects*. Int. J. Environ. Res. Public Health 2017, 14(7), 770; doi:10.3390/ijerph14070770

Intrigued, Dr. Lorenzen started an elaborate research into water. After he did a rigorously analysis of the work of past scientists, he tried to look not at "what is in the water" from chemical or scientifically point of view, but at "the water" itself.

He developed a way of flash-freezing water right at the source of the spring, by using liquid nitrogen. He brought the frozen samples of water back to the laboratory, where he performed detailed analyses (including X-ray and crystallography).

What he discovered is (again) pretty cool: the water from the healing spring presented structured geometric rings (micro-clusters) smaller than one's found in regular tap water. After analysing water from different sources, he realized that in all water bodies (springs, rivers, lakes or waterfalls) found in unpolluted areas, water comes in smaller clusters, than the polluted, or regular tap water. Although he presented very significant data about his findings to universities and research facilities in the United States (and he even applied for two patents, *Microclustered Water* and *Process for preparing microclustered water*), as in the case of the French Prof. Benveniste, his researches were dismissed, on the basis that such claims are impossible. Sad, but true.

Dr. Lorenzen is among the first ones who discovered that water comes in micro-clusters, but not the only one. In 1992, Professor Dr. S. Katayama, from the University of Shizuoka, School of Pharmaceutical Science, published a paper[40], in which he showed that small clustered water is the dominant form in very young, potent cells. It is more "active", assisting more in nutrient delivery, or waste removal, through the cell membrane.

In the human bodies, as we age, cell water mobility dramatically slows. Dr. Katayama determined that in a young, healthy child, water accounts for approx. 70% of the body weight, with a 60/40 ratio of intracellular water to extracellular water.

The dominant type of water is more "active", more "mobile", in the form of clustered water molecules. In an average middle-aged adult, the total body moisture content drops to 50% total body water, with a ratio of 50/50 intracellular moisture to extracellular moisture. Water is far more bound and less mobile. And, by the time we reach the age of 65, the average total body water accounts for only 45% of our body weight (or even lower), with a ratio of 40/60 intracellular to extracellular moisture. Thus, very little "active" water.

---

[40] Katayama S, *Aging mechanism associated with a function of biowater*, Physiol Chem Phys Med NMR. 1992;24(1):43-50. PMID: 1594660

Today, these are not news for the scientific community. It is an established fact that, due to partial covalence of water's hydrogen bonding, electrons are not held by individual molecules. They are instead distributed amongst water clusters. We can picture a water cluster as an enclosed circle of water molecules, with a very tiny size of 0.1 μm (meaning 10^{-6} meters, or one-millionth of a meter)[41].

The really cool part about water and its clusters is that gives rise to coherent regions, capable of interacting with electromagnetic radiations (meaning that inside that little tiny "circle", while regular matter cannot get in, anything electromagnetic can). This fact was proved since two decades ago by Dr. Lorenzen, and now, more recently, by Dr. Pollack's *EZ water*, Prof. Dr. Monagnier, and countless other scientists.[42,43,44,45,46,47]

Basically, what's important to remember is that water interacts with electromagnetism.

Now, if we go back inside the human body, we'll find a major organ, without which we couldn't experience the reality the way we do (unique for every one of us). This organ develops even before the pregnancy test comes back positive, and, in an adult person, is located in the most protected part of the body and has a water content of 73%. As you probably already guessed, I'm talking about the human brain.

Now, there are a lot of interesting findings regarding the human brain, and I will list some of them.

[41] I. Bono, E. Del Giudice, L. Gamberale, M. Henry, *Emergence of Quantum Coherence in Liquid Water and Aqueous Systems*, WATER 2012, 4(3), 510-532; doi:10.3390/w4030510

[42] L. Montagnier, J. Aïssa, S. Ferris, J.-L. Montagnier, C. Lavallée, *Electromagnetic signals are produced by aqueous nanostructures derived from bacterial DNA sequences*, Interdisciplinary Sciences: Computational Life Sciences, 1 (2009) 81-90; L. Montagnier, J. Aissa, E. Del Giudice, C. Lavallee, A. Tedeschi and G. Vitiello, *DNA waves and water*, Journal of Physics.: Conference Series, 306 (2011) 012007, arXiv:1012.5166v1 [q-bio.OT]

[43] J. G. Watterson, *Does solvent structure underlie osmotic mechanisms?*, Physical Chemistry Liq. vol. 16, 1987, issue 4, pp. 313-316

[44] Del Giudice E, Fuchs ED and Vitiello G (2010). *Collective molecular dynamics of a floating water bridge*. WATER Journal 2: 69-82

[45] Ho M.W. *Large Supramolecular Water Clusters Caught on Camera*, WATER Journal 6 (2013): http://dx.doi.org/10.14294/WATER.2013.12

[46] E. Del Giudice, V. Voeikov, A. Tedeschi and G. Vitiello, *The origin and the special role of coherent water in living systems*, Edition: Fields of the Cell, 2015, pp 95-111, Research Signpost 37/661, ISBN: 978-81-308-0544-3, DOI: 10.13140/RG.2.1.2329.1046

[47] L. Montagnier, J. Aïssa, S. Ferris, J.-L. Montagnier, C. Lavallée, *Electromagnetic signals are produced by aqueous nanostructures derived from bacterial DNA sequences*, Interdisciplinary Sciences: Computational Life Sciences, 1 (2009) 81-90; L. Montagnier, J. Aissa, E. Del Giudice, C. Lavallee, A. Tedeschi and G. Vitiello, *DNA waves and water*, Journal of Physics.: Conference Series, 306 (2011) 012007, arXiv:1012.5166v1 [q-bio.OT]

For example, as opposed to the old belief that the brain cells we were born with are the brain cells we will die with, in the past decades' neuroscientists discovered that our brain is growing new neurons.[48] This basically means that the brain we woke up in one morning is not identical with the brain we are going to sleep with at night. Another interesting fact is that the new neurons are growth particularly in response to traumas, and the brain has the ability to rearrange the way the neurons are communicating. Moreover, by mapping the brain's neural activity and studying its neurocircuitry, neuroscientists discovered that any individual has the ability to change his brain and the way the neurons are communicating, simply by changing his way of thinking, his thoughts.

Now let's understand a little the human brain. It performs three types of activities: it's "thinking" thoughts, simulates and "feels" emotions, and runs physiological responses to those thoughts and feelings, by releasing hormones and neurotransmitters into the bloodstream. For example, every second of our day, the brain releases noradrenaline (or norepinephrine) in our bloodstream. Its chemical formula is $C_8H_{11}NO_3$ (look how the *water former* rules our life, to the smallest detail).

Noradrenaline release is lowest during sleep, rises during wakefulness, and reaches its highest levels during situations of stress or danger (in the so-called fight-or-flight response). Now, scientists discovered that it takes less than 90 seconds from the beginning of a thought (or feeling), until the moment our blood is cleaned from the chemistry released by the brain, as a response to that particular thought or feeling.[49] This is why we can't stay mad for more than 1 minute, and we are advised many times when we're angry to "take a deep breath and count until ten".

An adult brain is composed from about 100 billion nerve cells (called neurons) which are interconnected by trillions of connections (synapses), and performs thousands of trillions of operations per second. Each connection transmits, on average, about one electric impulse (signal) per second, although there are some specialized connections that can send up to 1,000 signals per second. In other words, every time we feel a breeze, we drink a glass of water or we eat some food, when we see some images on the TV, we hear some words in an advertisement, we pick up a part of a conversation at the office or in a restaurant, each of these events are triggering a series of electric signals in the brain.

---

[48] Purves D, Augustine GJ, Fitzpatrick D, et al., editors. Neuroscience. 2nd edition. Sunderland (MA): Sinauer Associates; 2001. Generation of Neurons in the Adult Brain. Available from: https://www.ncbi.nlm.nih.gov/books/NBK10920/
[49] Dr. Jill Bolte Taylor, *The Neuroanatomical Transformation of the Teenage Brain*, TEDxYouth@Indianapolis, Feb 21, 2013, approx. min 2:38-2:44 of 16:30

Moreover, the brain has to keep up with the internal activity, since thousands of chemical reactions are taking place in the same time in our body's cells. Our ability to remember things, to solve problems, to coordinate and balance our body, to breathe or to digest, they're all performed through electromagnetic impulses.

These electromagnetic impulses are measurable through electroencephalography (EEG), and (as another interesting fact) scientists discovered that in its awake state, the brain generates enough electricity to power a light bulb. But, don't get too excited that you could lower your electric bill, because the electromagnetic field generated by the brain is very small compared with other electric appliances, and, since is easily distorted by any other electromagnetic fields nearby, loses all its potency.

But, enough with the brain. Let's see what other major organ we have inside our body. And there's another one, located inside the chest, almost as protected as the brain in the case of an external injury. Same as the brain, without it, the "water machine" we call human body could not exist. In fact, is the first organ that emerges from water, starting to develop when the embryo is only 2 - 3 mm long, in the first 15 to 21 days after conception.[50]

You got it. I am talking about the human heart, which is known as the muscular organ that pumps blood through the blood vessels of the circulatory system. Yet, if we look at the "electric circuit" of the human body from water's perspective, we notice that in an adult person, the brain, the heart, the spinal cord and the nerve trunks, they all have the same amount of water: about 73%.

Moreover, in my opinion, heart's importance is equal (if not higher) with that of the brain. Although the majority regards the heart merely as a simple muscular organ that pumps blood throughout the body, since the blood (made of 92% water) carries around the nutrients and the waste products (and more important, the oxygen needed to survive), if the "pump" fails, there would be no blood, thus no oxygen, so basically, no life. It's pretty simple. Luckily, doctors figured out how to "reset the pump" and "restart the machine", by applying an electric shock (with the help of a defibrillator), which briefly stops the activity of the heart, allowing it to return to its normal rhythm.

From the Cardiology approach, the heart is a "pump", while from the Fluid Mechanics' perspective, the blood vessels are a bunch of interconnected ducts (known in Medicine as arteries, veins, arterioles, capillaries and venules), with different lengths and diameters. Inside these

---

[50] J-Marc Schleich, *Development of the human heart: days 15–21*, Heart. 2002 May; 87(5): 487. PMCID: PMC1767109

pipelines runs some fluid (the human blood, which is made of about 92% water), which has some characteristics: pressure, viscosity, and, since we're talking about the blood vessels, vascular resistance.

Of course, we know from Physics that water (the main component of the fluid that runs inside our bodies) has the highest heat capacity of all other liquids, the greatest surface tension of any liquid (other than mercury), has a capillary action (manifesting the highest cohesive force of all non-metallic liquids), and of course, it is the *"universal solvent"*. However, these properties are not really taken into account when scientists are referring to the blood flow. Since it's just a "simple" fluid that runs through a pipeline, water's pressure, viscosity, and resistance is pretty much all that counts.

When the pipelines are accumulating too much rust on their internal walls, the fluid (the blood) doesn't flow at the same pressure. A change in the pressure of a fluid means... well... for sure you ran out of water at home at least once in your lifetime.

Far from me to argue that Cardiology or Mechanics approaches are wrong. Yet, in my opinion, I find the Physics and Thermodynamics takes much more interesting.

From Thermodynamics perspective we can picture the human body as a system (picture it like a tightly closed jar filled with water molecules), which continuously exchanges heat (energy) with the surrounding environment, in order to keep a constant internal temperature of about 37 °C (or 98.6 °F).

Now, truth is that all organic life and health is based on very subtle differences in temperature. For example, our Blue Planet is located in the so-called Goldilocks Zone (the habitable zone around a star where the temperature is just right, not too hot and not too cold, for liquid water to exist), while we, as "water machines", we begin to sweat, or shiver, if our body temperature rises/drops by as little as 0.5°C (0.9°F).

From Physics approach, we might say that our heart and our brain are like little "power cells": they both start emitting and receiving electromagnetic impulses long before we are emerging from water (we're coming out from the amniotic fluid), and they're both with us till the day we leave this Blue Planet. If any of these "power cells" fails, well... you know what's happening (or, at least you think you know).

As I mentioned in the preface, we cannot truly understand water, by looking at it only from the scientific point of view. Thus, let's return for a second back to our forefathers' beliefs, and see what was their belief about the human heart.

Actually, if we'd "travel back in time" for a shorter period, we encounter one of the greatest inventors of the past millennium, Leonardo da Vinci (1452-1519). Although not a scientists per se, he was one of the "leading lights" of the Italian Renaissance, and manifested interest in painting, sculpting, architecture, science, music, mathematics, engineering, anatomy, geology, astronomy, botany, writing, history, and cartography.

Leonardo's vision about our Blue Planet was quite different. He wrote in his Notebooks that *"nothing grows in a spot where there is neither sentient, fibrous nor rational life. The feathers grow upon birds and change every year; hair grows upon animals and changes every year except a part such as the hair of the beard in lions and cats and creatures like these. The grass grows in the fields, the leaves upon the trees, and every year these are renewed in great part. So then we may say that the earth has a spirit of growth, and that its flesh is the soil; its bones are the successive strata of the rocks which form the mountains; its cartilage is the tufa stone; its blood the springs of its waters. The lake of blood that lies about the heart is the ocean. Its breathing is by the increase and decrease of the blood in its pulses, and even so in the earth is the ebb and flow of the sea.'*[51]

That's right. Da Vinci believed that our Earth is a living being (and I'll like to mention that he wasn't the only one, there are many other famous inventors and philosophers that had the same opinion). For Da Vinci, the springs of waters represented our Blue Planet's blood, while its heart was the oceans. Sounds crazy, right?

Well, same were his inventions. The parachute (invented with hundreds of years before humanity was able to fly), snowshoes to walk on water, breathing devices and webbed gloves to explore underwater, scuba gear, the helical air screw (similar to today's helicopters), self-propelled cart (capable of moving without being pushed, powered by coiled springs, featuring also steering and brake capabilities) and many others.

All these with no formal academic training. He grew up in rural Tuscany and spent much of his time outdoors, and he never received any kind of formal education, except for his basic teachings from home, in subjects such as reading, writing and some mathematics.

But let's travel a little further in our past, and see what was our forefathers' general approach regarding the human heart. Since ancient times, they associated it with the source of emotions, courage and wisdom. For example, ancient Egyptians believed that the emotions and intellect arose from the heart. The Chinese associated it with the centre of happiness, while Aristotle believed that the heart was the seat of intelligence, containing all emotions

[51] *The Notebooks of Leonardo da Vinci*, Arranged, Rendered into English and Introduced by Edward MacCurdy, New York, George Braziller, 1955, p. 86

and thinking. In fact, even today, when we see somebody doing some good things, we say that he has *"good heart"*, or whenever we have to make a difficult decision, the first advice we hear is *"follow your heart"*.

Well, again, it seems that these ancient beliefs are not so far from the truth. And here's why…

In 1991, Dr. J. Andrew Armour, M.D., Ph.D., from the University of Montreal, introduced a new concept in the medical community: the "heart-brain".

According to Dr. Armour, *"it has become clear in recent years that a sophisticated two-way communication occurs between the heart and brain, with each influencing the other's function."*[52]

Moreover, *"in the last ten years, evidence has accumulated for the presence of a functional heart brain — first described as the "little brain on the heart." From a neuroscience perspective, the nervous system within the heart, that is intrinsic to the heart, is made up of populations of neurons capable of processing information independent of extracardiac neurons (including those in the CNS).*[53]

In simple terms, our heart has its own brain. This fact was further confirmed by scientific studies made at the HeartMath Institute, which showed that the human heart has its own nervous system, composed of approximately 40,000 neurons, that can all sense, feel, learn and remember.

These neurons are connected differently and more elaborate than elsewhere in the body, and, while they are capable of detecting circulating chemicals sent from the brain and other organs, they operate independently in their own right. This means that our heart can be influenced by messages sent from the brain, but it does not necessarily obey them all the time.

Furthermore, the heart's "little-brain" sends more information to the brain than the brain sends to the heart and exercises its own influence on the brain.

And, when it comes about electromagnetism, scientists had recently caught up with the ancient beliefs concerning the body's aura (or the auric field) and they discovered that the heart produces the largest electromagnetic field of the body's organs.

As opposed to the electromagnetic field generated by the brain (which can be measured only in the skull area), the electrical impulses that move through our heart can be detected anywhere on the surface of the body, and can be traced with the help of an electrocardiogram.

---

[52] Dr. J. Andrew Armour, M.D., Ph.D., *Neurocardiology: Anatomical & Functional Principles*, Published by the Institute of HeartMath, 2003, pg. 1
[53] Ibid. pg. 5

Furthermore, by using SQUID (superconducting quantum interference device)-based magnetometers, scientists determined that the magnetic field produced by the heart is about 60 times greater in amplitude than the electrical activity generated by the brain, and more than 100 times greater in strength, being detected up to 1 meter (c. 3 feet) away from the body, in all directions.[54]

In the ancient beliefs, the Aura (or, in modern terms, the heart's electromagnetic field) was associated with vitality, mental clarity, health and emotional well-being, as well as highly positive spiritual energies flowing through a person. In the case of a healthy person, the auric field is wider and brighter, and vice versa, appears depleted in cases of unhealthy or unbalanced persons.

And here's another interesting finding: it seems that the heart has the ability to store our personality, and even transmit that information in case of a transplant. In 2000, a team of researchers from the University of Hawaii and University of Arizona published a study[55] in which they describe the evaluation (through a series of open-ended interviews) of 10 individuals who received a heart or heart-lung transplants. The interviews involved transplant recipients, recipient families or friends, and donor families or friends, in hospitals, in various parts of the US.

Researchers investigated several parallels, including changes in food, music, art, sexual, recreational, and career preferences, and also specific instances of perceptions of names and sensory experiences related to the donors. From the case of a vegetarian health-conscious donor, which turned a McDonalds-loving recipient into a straight vegetarian who hated meat after the transplant, to the case of a 18-year-old girl who was a "hell-raiser" and ended picking up her donor's love for music and poetry, the study shows a very high transfer of personality traits, that immunosuppressant drugs, stress of surgery, or statistical coincidence cannot explain.

If you want, you can take a look over the study, I placed it in the footnotes, and is available on the internet. I found it pretty interesting, and, in fact, I found interesting and worth of sharing all the all the information that I gathered in this booklet, else I wouldn't have wasted my time with writing it. But let's move on to another study, regarding emotions.

---

[54] https://www.heartmath.org/research/science-of-the-heart/energetic-communication/
[55] Paul Pearsall, Gary E.R. Schwartz, Linda G.S. Russek, Changes in Heart Transplant Recipients that Parallel the Personalities of their Donors, *Integrative Medicine*, Vol. 2, No. 2. (2000), pp. 65-72, https://doi.org/10.1016/S1096-2190(00)00013-5

In 2014 scientists published the results of a research, according to which the emotions do tend to be felt in all our bodies in ways that are generally consistent from one person to the next, irrespective of age, sex, or nationality. This shouldn't come as a surprise, now that we know that we are more 99.9% identical from DNA point of view, or that we are mostly water, and we're all connected through the electromagnetic fields (or the aura). Here's a cool picture from this particular study:

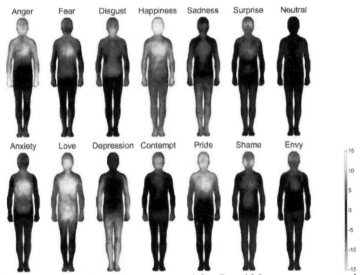

Bodily maps of emotions (Image copyright: Lauri Nummenmaa, et al. *Proc. Natl. Acad. Sci.* USA, 2014[56])

And there's another thing. Scientists discovered **that while negative emotions can create nervous system chaos, positive emotions can increase the brain's ability to make good decisions. Our heart electromagnetic field is changing according to our emotions!** (You didn't see this coming, although you experience it countless times: every time you're stressed or angry, the decisions you make turn out to be not the most brilliant ones. Of course, most are blaming someone else for their own decisions, and is always somebody else's fault, but that's another thing.

But wait... there's more. Scientists proved that **the quality of our emotions, through the electromagnetic energy radiating from our heart can be picked up not only by others** (that's why people from a party are getting depressed when somebody who's not in the mood walks in), **but also by plants and animals.**

---

[56] http://www.pnas.org/content/111/2/646.figures-only

Now, if we remember that water is influenced by the electromagnetic forces, and water is found not only inside our bodies, but all around us in the surrounding environment, you're starting to see the big picture, right?

If not, let's take a look at more photos, because, as the old proverb goes, a picture is worth a thousand words.

One of the first who captured the influence of the electromagnetic fields upon water was a Japanese Doctor in Alternative Medicine, Dr. Masaru Emoto from the IHM Institute, Japan. For those interested in Dr. Emoto's life, and how he came up with the idea to photograph water crystals, I encourage you to make a little research and read his many books.

Dr. Emoto's general technique of photographing water crystals was quite simple: a specimen of water was frozen at -25°C (about -13°F) and then placed under a microscope, in a laboratory where the temperature was maintained constantly at -5°C (c. 23°F). As the temperature of the ice tip was rising, the water crystal was growing and expanding, allowing to be photographed in different stages.

According to Dr. Emoto, when he first captured the first successful photograph on frozen micro-clustered water (after about two months of trial and error), he was so moved that he shed tears of joy. For him was the confirmation that water reflects not only the physical word around it (kind of like a mirror, when we look into a placid lake or a pond), but also the consciousness of the beings surrounding it.

Here's Dr. Emoto's very first crystal photo, successfully photographed in 1994.

The very first crystal photo of *"resonant magnetic field water"* (Image copyright: IHM institute)[57]

---

[57] Image source: http://hado.com/ihm/subscription/frozen-water-crystal-photographs-2/

Same as Dr. Lorenzen before him, Dr. Emoto noticed that he couldn't get any beautiful crystals from tap water, or from rivers and lakes located near big cities. Conversely, he was capturing beautiful hexagonal crystals (each having its own uniqueness), in water from rivers and lakes kept pristine from human development.

This led him to two conclusions: that the hexagonal shape represents the life force of Mother Nature, and that the absence of the hexagonal crystals can be seen as a sign that the life forces in that area have been compromised energetically.

★ ★ ★ ★ ★ ★

"The hexagonal crystals represents the life force of Mother Nature."
Dr. Masaru Emoto (1943 – 2014)

★ ★ ★ ★ ★ ★

The first collection of his work was published in 1994, in *The truth of Hado*, followed in 1999 by the *Messages from water*, the world's first collection of water crystal photos.

While he was photographing water crystals from all over the world, Dr. Emoto thought that, since music is sound, and sound is vibration, water's crystal structure would change. It makes sense, since when we share our thoughts and feelings, we do that through words. Ok, only about 7% from what we're sending in the surrounding environment (or what others "hear") are words. The rest of 38% represents the use or certain vocal elements (including the intonation placed behind a word), while 55% consists of other non-verbal elements, like posture, gestures, facial expressions, and so on. Still, when we're expressing ourselves through words, these are leaving the mouth as sounds, which are traveling through air as forms of vibration, and become again "words" only after were captured by our interlocutor(s) ear(s), converted and interpreted by her, him, or them. While in air, our thoughts and feelings (expressed through words), are nothing more than forms of vibration. Same with the music and any other forms of sound we hear.

So, Dr. Emoto placed distilled water in front of two speakers, played different songs, and repeated the procedure of freezing the crystals. He proved to be right in his assumption, and he noticed changes in the crystal structure of the water. Here are few astonishing pictures with different crystals of water before, and after water "listened" some songs.

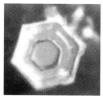

The crystal of distilled water, before being exposed to music[58].

Water crystals after water was exposed to music (Image copyright IHM Institute[59])

As we can see, the hexagonal crystal shape manifests its presence in many crystals. Dr. Emoto called this the *Hado* effect and described it as *"the intrinsic vibration pattern at the atomic level in all matter, the smallest unit of energy. Its basis is the energy of human consciousness"*.

Now, as a short parenthesis, I have to mention that there are some differences (and also similarities) between the Western and the Asiatic systems of beliefs. In the Western culture, scientists are trying to explain the world in mechanical terms, based on the general assumption that all things

---

[58] *Water Crystals in Motion – Messages From Water*, directed by I.H.M. General Institute, May 5, 2004 (approx. 15:46 of 43:03)
[59] Image source: http://www.emotopeaceproject.net/crystal-gallery/4584092360

can be taken apart and viewed at a smaller or closer level. Mainstream Western scientists believe that everything in the Universe can be perceived and explained by the human being (sort of *"seeing is believing"*, instead of *"believe and don't doubt"*, if you'd like). On the flip side, the Asian cultures recognized the science of energy for centuries. Techniques like *Reiki, Seitai, Qigong* or *acupuncture* are focused on energy rather than physical mass.

And as far as regarding similarities between the two major cultures, in both, the scientists agree that all substances and phenomena have their own unique electromagnetic resonance field. So, basically, *Hado* is the manifestation of a specific vibrating electromagnetic wave.

While performing the photographic experiments, Dr. Emoto started treating patients, using a Computerized Magnetic Resonance Analyser (MRA) and personalized homeopathic remedies made with micro-clustered water. He cured over 10,000 cases (many of them described in his books), and, according to a documentary film from the I.H.M Institute, by 2004, he counselled about 15,000 people.[60]

However, he encountered many cases when patients were living far away, or they were hospitalized. In these cases, Dr. Emoto asked the patients for a personal picture and their symptoms, and with the help of the MRA, he created individual *Hado* water for each patient, treating (as incredible as it might sound) many cases without the patient's physical presence.

This led Dr. Emoto to another idea. He thought that if the photograph of a person can provide information to water, maybe his name could do the same thing.

By the way, the fact that words (as sounds traveling through air, or in their written form, have a very significant importance) wasn't a secret for our forefathers. This can be noticed at a close reading, from a slightly scientific angle, of the verses found in the beginning of the Old and New Testament. In the Book of Genesis we read that *"God said, Let there be light..."* (Genesis 1:3), *"And God said, Let there be a firmament in the midst of the waters..."* (Genesis 1:6); *"And God said, Let the waters under the heaven be gathered together..."* (Genesis 1:9); *"And God said, Let the earth bring forth grass..."* (Genesis 1:11); *"And God said, Let there be lights in the firmament of the heaven..."* (Genesis 1:14); *"And God said, Let us make man in our image..."* (Genesis 1:26), while is the New Testament, the very first verses we read are *"In the beginning was the Word, and the Word was with God, and the Word was God."* (John 1:1).

---

[60] *Water Crystals in Motion – Messages From Water*, directed by I.H.M. General Institute, May 5, 2004 (approx. 3:10 and approx. 22:00 of 43:03)

But let's stay in Japan for now and see what Dr. Emoto discovered. He measured the *Hado* of his patient's name and realized that written words retain vibrational information. So, he started to expose water to various written words, to different photos and to various substances found in nature. Each and every time, water seemed to collect and retain the information to which was exposed.[61]

Here's for example the difference in the water crystals when we think (or we write on a piece of paper) that "we can" or "we can't" do something:

I can't do it · I can do it

Image copyright IHM Institute

Inspired by Dr. Emoto's work, a student from an elementary school set up an experiment: she placed cooked rice into two glass jars, and for 30 days, she said "thank you" to one container, and "you fool" to the other. At the end of the month, the rice from the jar that was told "thank you" developed a rich and pleasant smell, while the rice from the other container turned black, with mould, starting to emit a foul odour.

Rice experiment (image source Masaru Emoto, *The Message from Water, Children's version*[62])

---

[61] http://www.masaru-emoto.net/english/water-crystal.html
[62] http://www.emotopeaceproject.net/picture-books/4584092537

Dr. Emoto and his team from the IHM Institute repeated the experiment by using three glass beakers instead of two. They said "Thank You" to the rice in the first beaker, "You are an idiot" to the second, and they completely ignored the third container.

After one month, the rice from the first beaker began to ferment, giving a strong, pleasant aroma. The rice from the second beaker turned black, while the rice from the third one started to rot.

Dr. Emoto concluded that this experiment provides an important lesson, especially on how we treat our children: *"We should take care of them, give them attention, and converse with them. Indifference does the greatest harm. It may not always be easy to do, and, almost always, it takes practice".*[63]

* * * * * *

"To give your positive or negative attention to something is a way of giving energy. The most damaging form of behaviour is withholding your attention."
Dr. Masaru Emoto (1943 – 2014)
* * * * * *

The experiment gained popularity among Dr. Emoto's readers and was repeated by many others, on different types of rice, and even on plants and flowers.

Yet, an interesting thing happened among Dr. Emoto's critics. As in the case of the DARPA failed attempt to recreate Dr. Benveniste's experiments regarding "water memory", many of Dr. Emoto's sceptics reported no results after performing the experiment.

Same thing was noticed in Germany, at the Institute of Statics and Dynamics of Aerospace Structures, at Stuttgart University, where a team conducted by Prof. Dr. Bernd Kröplin performed similar researches. They placed stones, metals, and even twigs and flowers into the water. By photographing the water crystals, they proved that water has the ability to receive and retain the information to which it was exposed.

For example, in an experiment called "lettuce listening to a mobile phone", the team of scientists filled up with tap water a big pot, in which they placed a head of lettuce. They photographed the ice crystal of the reference water (the tap water from the Institute), and its crystal revealed in the middle of the drop a dark spot. However, after coming in contact with the lettuce,

---

[63] Russian documentary *"Вода" (Water)*, written by Saida Medvedeva and Sergey Shumakov, directed by Julia Perkul and Anastasiya Popova, released in Russia and USA in 2008 (approx.52:33-52:50 of 1:23:16).

the dark spot disappeared, revealing instead a bright centre. According to Dr. Kröplin, this is a very often phenomenon, which occurs after tap water comes in contact with living things (yes, including plants).

In the second experiment, the researchers placed another head of lettuce next to a mobile phone which they turned it on for two minutes. As expected, the lettuce absorbed the electromagnetic radiation emitted by the phone. Here are the pictures from the experiment:

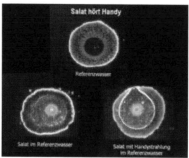

The "lettuce listening to a mobile phone" experiment (Up – picture of the reference water; Bottom left – picture of the same water after a head of lettuce was placed in the water; Bottom right – picture of the reference water, after the lettuce was exposed to electromagnetic radiations)[64].

However, Dr. Kröplin got intrigued by an anomaly that occurred during the experiments. Drops from the same water revealed different images depending on the individual who was handling the experiment. Therefore, he asked different students to place, in the same time, drops from the same water, on the testing sheet. After he photographed the ice crystals, the results were surprising: each individual produced different images.

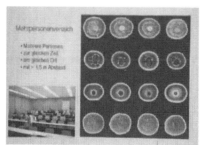

Images produced by different students from the same water[65]

[64]Image compilation: screen capture from the documentary film "Unser Wissen ist ein Tropfen - Wasser, das unbekannte Wesen" ("What We Know is a Drop: The Mystery of Water"), directed by Hans Kronberger and Gundi Lamprecht, Austria, 2008
[65] Ibid.

On the right side, from top to bottom, we can see the images produced by four different students from the same water. Dr. Kröplin concluded that the experimenter who is holding the syringe and has never been in direct physical contact with the water, somehow transfers personal information to the water. This information is captured by the water and revealed by the crystal photograph.

Hopefully, the proverb "a picture is worth a thousand words" worked in this case, and I like to think that you got the point and you understand how every single thought, feeling and intention is impacting the water, both inside and outside a person's body. And, in my opinion, the explanation why DARPA's experiments didn't succeed, or why many people failed in replicating the "rice experiment" (while many others succeeded) is because their intentions were not so, let's call them, pure and kind, and I sure hope you will agree with me by the end of the book.

If we really think about our thoughts and feelings from the electromagnetic perspective, we realize that they have a tremendous impact. Since water captures the electromagnetic fields, this means that a person's thoughts and feelings are influencing not only what's happening in his own body but also in the surrounding environment.

Every uttered word (and even the written words), every sound we make, every thought and every emotion are forms of vibration, that causes our heart and our brain to generate electrical impulses. These electrical impulses are carried all over our bodies, affecting the water's structure on every level, starting from our cells and internal organs to the whole Universe. That's right, even it might sound a little too far out for most of the readers.

Actually, Viktor Schauberger (1885 – 1958), another brilliant inventor and naturalist (who also believed that water is the supreme source and invented back in the 1930s what many refer today as the UFO), said that *"Today's science thinks too primitively; indeed it could be said that its thinking is an octave too low. It has still not ventured far enough into the realm of energy, and its attitude has remained purely materialistic. For this reason, it is principally to blame for the state of affairs we are experiencing today."*

And here's another favourite quote, this time from the His Holiness Tenzin Gyatso, the 14th Dalai Lama of Tibetan Buddhism:

* * * * * *

"Just as ripples spread out when a single pebble is dropped into water, the actions of individuals can have far-reaching effects."

* * * * * *

But let's analyse more cases. However, before we start, let me mention that this "wild idea" that we are all connected, and *the actions of individuals can have far reaching effects"* is not a new concept in the scientific community.

For example, many of you remember the 2008 financial crisis that started in the USA. It is considered the worst economic crisis since the 1930s Great Depression. A contiguous chain of events (actions, causes and effects), which linked together, affected the economies of many countries, from all over the world. In Chemistry and Thermodynamics, we know the phenomenon as 'chain reaction', a sequence of reactions where a reactive product or by-product causes additional reactions to take place. In Mechanics is known as the 'domino effect', a cumulative effect produced when one event sets off a chain of similar events (the term being used as an analogy to a falling row of dominoes). The 'butterfly effect', a term coined by the American mathematician and meteorologist Edward Norton Lorenz, and derived from the metaphorical example of the details of a tornado (the exact time of formation, the exact path taken) being influenced by minor perturbations such as the flapping of the wings of a distant butterfly several weeks earlier. Or the 'snowball effect' – the process that starts from an initial state of small significance and builds upon itself, becoming larger, graver and more serious –, associated with the rolling of a snowball down a snow-covered hillside. As it rolls, the ball picks up more snow, gains more mass and surface area, picking up even more snow and momentum as it rolls along. And many other examples.

Now, let's take a look at some more pictures to see how far our sincere intentions, thoughts and feelings are reaching into the surrounding environment.

On January 17, 1995, Japan was hit by an earthquake (the Hanshin Awaji earthquake) which measured 6.9 on the moment magnitude scale, and 7 on the JMA Shindo intensity scale. Although the initial tremors lasted for approximately 20 seconds, aftershocks strong enough to be felt lasted more than 70 days.

Sadly, over 6,000 people lost their lives, more than 60 children under the age of 18 were orphaned, while over 300 additional children lost one parent. Nearly 400,000 buildings suffered irreparably damages and over half of the houses in the southern part of Hyōgo Prefecture were deemed unfit to live in. Many elevated road and rail bridges, highways, railways and subways were damaged, as well as 120 of the 150 quays in the port of Kobe. As in any natural disaster, Kobe's southern part of Hyōgo Prefecture suffered disruptions of water, electricity and gas supplies.

Three days after this tragic disaster, Dr. Masaru Emoto collected samples from the tap water, and its photographs revealed a completely destroyed crystal, like as if water captured the fear, panic and deep sorrow of the people immediately after the earthquake.

In the following 3 months, approximately 1.2 million volunteers were involved in relief efforts. Multiple national and international retailers and companies used their existing supply networks to provide necessities in affected areas or provided free telephone service for victims, and, according to an article published by the Japan Policy Research Institute, even the members of *Yakuza* (Japan's transnational organized crime syndicates) were involved in distributing food and supplies to needy victims.[66]

When the people restored their environment due to the helping hands and sympathy from all over the world (three months later after the disaster), Dr. Emoto collected some other samples of water. It turned out that the crystals seemed to have collected the community feelings, restoring their beautiful hexagonal shape.[67]

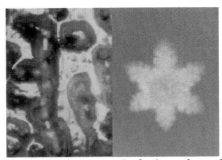

Water crystals from Kobe tap water. Left: three days after the Hanshin Awaji earthquake; Right: three months after the earthquake.
(Image copyright: Masaru Emoto, Image source: *Messages from water*, p. 130)

On February 2, 1997, Dr. Emoto performed another experiment: he asked 500 graduates of his *Hado* courses to transmit simultaneously their feelings, from all over Japan.

"At 2:00 on February 2, 1997, I will leave a cup containing tap water of Shinagawa-ku on the table in my office. Please transmit your feelings to that water at the same time all over Japan. Of course, for this water to become a clean water, please send "Chi and Soul" of love and the wish that the water should become clean. Thank you very much.", wrote Dr. Emoto in his letter.

---

[66] Andrew Morse and Todd Zaun, *"Views from Two Observers"* and Robert M. Orr, Jr., *"The Relief Effort Seen by a Participant"*, JPRI Occasional Paper No. 2 (March 1995).
[67] Masaru Emoto, *Messages from water*, Seventh Issue, First edition, August 15, 2000, published by HADO Kyoikusha, translated by TMS Communications Ltd.

Although almost nobody believed that they can perform a clear change in the condition of the water, the image obtained revealed a beautiful hexagonal shaped crystal.[68]

Crystal of tap water from the Shinagawa-ku, Tokyo, after 500 people transmitted the "Chi and Soul" of love, from all over Japan (Image copyright: IHM Institute[69]).

Another example is found in the case from the Fujiwara dam lake, where a Buddhist monk (Reverend Kato Hoki, chief priest of Jyuhouin Temple, Omiya City), cleansed in 1997 the dirty dam water.

After about 1 hour of prayers and incantations, water started to clear up, and finally, by the end of the ceremony, even the vegetation from the bottom of the lake become visible. [70]

Well, I have to admit, Reverend Hoki's spiritual power is pretty strong. Just look at how the water crystal changed:

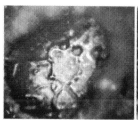

Water crystal from the Fujiwara dam lake.
Left: before the prayer; Right: After Kato Hoki's prayer.
(Image copyright: Masaru Emoto, Dr. Emoto's official blog[71]).

---

[68] Ibid., page 131

[69] Image source: Emoto Peace Project website (emotopeaceproject.net)/Crystal Gallery/Water exposed to prayer (http://www.emotopeaceproject.net/crystal-gallery/4584092360)

[70] Masaru Emoto, "My sincere request to the concerned people in the world", Dr. Emoto's official blog – Messages from water, posted on March 8, 2013

[71] Ibid.

In another case, in the early morning of July 25th, 1999, Dr. Emoto asked a large crowd of people to project their positive intentions onto the polluted waters of the Lake Biwa (the biggest lake of Japan). More than 300 people hold a ceremony that lasted few days, and at the end of the ceremony, the local newspaper reported that suddenly there were no longer bad odours emitting from the lake.

But let me point out some intriguing observations. For example, it seems that water understands the meaning behind a written word, and not only the word itself. It captures its essence, the real thought, feeling or intention that lies behind the word. Is like the water doesn't recognize the word as a simple design, rather "understands" the meaning behind the word, and changes its crystal accordingly.

Let's take a look at the English word "Thank You". In German is written as "Danke", in France is "Merci", and so on…(there are about 7,000 written languages on our collective home, the one and only Blue Planet which we call Earth; in fact, if somebody would visit our planet coming from space, he would call it "Water", instead of "Earth", because more than 70% of our Blue Planet is covered with water).

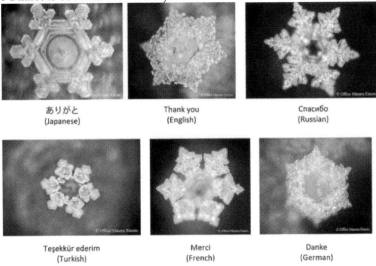

ありがと (Japanese)	Thank you (English)	Спасибо (Russian)
Teşekkür ederim (Turkish)	Merci (French)	Danke (German)

Water crystals after being exposed to the word "Thank You" in different languages (Image copyright: IHM Institute)[72]

---

[72] Image source: IHM Institute, Masaru Emoto's Hado world, http://hado.com/ihm/subscription/new-photos/

Dr. Emoto took pictures on the water crystals even after water was exposed to the name of the five major religions. The results were astonishing.

| Christianity | Islam | Hinduism |
| Buddhism | Judaism | All five religions |

The character of each religion shown by water
(image copyright: IHM Institute)[73]

We can clearly see the shape of the harmonious crystals, capturing the essence and the teachings of every religion. In dr. Emoto's opinion, this shows us that no religion is better than the other, and no religion is more right than another.

In his book *"Secret Life of Water"*, Dr. Emoto concluded that the five major religions can be united in one faith, *"a religion for the soul"* as he called him, but this thing is possible only with the will and the cooperation of the humankind.

---

[73]   Image   source: IHM   Institute,   Masaru   Emoto's   Hado   world,
http://hado.com/ihm/subscription/frozen-water-crystal-photographs-2/

Here are some more pictures, in which we can clearly see the difference between other positive and negative words.

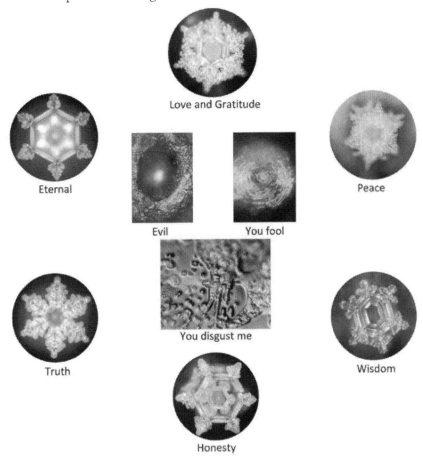

Water crystals after exposed to various positive and negative words
(Image copyright: IHM Institute, Office Masaru Emoto)[74]

★ ★ ★ ★ ★ ★

"We can change our minds. We don't have to give in to anger and hatred. Since compassion and anger cannot co-exist, the more we cultivate compassion the more our anger will be reduced."
His Holiness Tenzin Gyatso, 14th Dalai Lama

★ ★ ★ ★ ★ ★

[74] Image source: Office Masaru Emoto official website/ Water Crystals: http://www.masaru-emoto.net/english/water-crystal.html

In Dr. Emoto's opinion, if our thoughts, feelings, and intentions (prayers) are pure, we can change the material reality by using water as a medium. In fact, by using the collective power of the prayer, Dr. Emoto performed many water ceremonies, all over the world (from Florida, USA to Lake Baikal in Russia, in Colombia, Tokyo, Hawaii, Mexico, Taiwan or Liechtenstein).[75]

After he studied the resulted crystals, Dr. Emoto came up with a new, unusual formula for water. By replacing the *"water-former"* (hydrogen) with the word Gratitude, and the oxygen with Love, Dr. Emoto concluded that we need two parts of Gratitude and one part of Love in order to achieve balance.

So far, the information presented is pretty cool; you got to admit it. However, let's return for a moment to the beginning and to our forefathers' beliefs. Let's "complete the circle", if you'd like.

All the scientific findings presented in this book regarding our emotions and feelings are not something that our ancestors were unfamiliar with. In fact, we encounter even nowadays countless wise proverbs in the folklore from all around the world that mention "the power of love". There is the French proverb *"Nothing is impossible for a willing heart"*. The Greeks are saying that *"The heart that loves is always young"*. In the Indian tradition *"Where love reigns, the impossible may be attained"*. In Burundi *"Where there is love, there is no darkness"*. *"Love has to be shown by deeds, not words"* in Swahili. In Italy *"Love rules without rules"*. In the Chinese philosophy *"A flower cannot blossom without sunshine nor a garden without love"*. *"A woman prefers poverty with love to wealth without love"* in Hebrew tradition. And, perhaps the most encountered ones, all around the world, *"You can't buy love"* and *"Love will find a way"*.

At the same time, in our everyday life we see many examples in which persons who think they are *'in love'* perform reckless actions. In some cases, they're changing into completely different people, ignoring the advice of their family and close friends, becoming dishonest, and even lying and doing irrational things, in the name of the person they believe are *'in love'* with. This can be easily observed in both genres, being a little more prevalent in women than in men. Sadly, in almost all the cases, their partner takes advantage of their trust/naivety, thus we the world-spread famous proverb, *"Love is blind!"*

So, what's up with this thing? How can we achieve everything through Love, and still, Love to be blind?

---

[75] Emoto Peace Project website (emotopeaceproject.net)/Water Ceremony: http://www.emotopeaceproject.net/water-ceremony/4584092466

Thing is (and we're getting close to the end of the book with this last journey into the human body), that the connection between the electromagnetic signals transmitted by our heart and the ones generated in the brain is taking place in a part of the brain called corpus callosum, a bundle of nerve tissue containing an estimate of about 300 million axons (nerve fibres that carry electrical impulses from neuron's cell bodies).

See, the human brain is divided down the middle into two hemispheres and the connection between these two hemispheres is made by corpus callosum, which is responsible for transmitting neural messages (electrical impulses) between both the right and left hemispheres.

Now, scientists found out that each half of the brain is performing a distinct set of operations. While the left hemisphere uses logic and reason, identifying with the individual (me, me, me, and only me), the right hemisphere uses emotions and intuition, identifying with the group (we, instead of me).

The left hemisphere thinks linearly and methodically. It categorizes and organizes the information received from the internal and external stimuli, associates it with everything that is already memorized from the past, and projects into the future all of our possibilities. The left hemisphere operates ("thinks") sequentially, in language (words), and deals with parts and specifics. It's a kind of super-cool computer, which has in it the recordings of all our memories (since we first opened our eyes on this wonderful Blue Planet, and beyond), our dreams, past events and future plans.

On the other hand, the right hemisphere "thinks" in pictures, sounds, colours, synthesizes and puts together all the information, and deals with wholes and relationships. Now take a wild guess which one's more developed in males and which one in women. That's right, the right hemisphere is more developed in women, that's why they are more religious and loving than men (generally speaking).

Now, let's take a peek inside the corpus callosum. We'll find one of the endocrine glands (endocrine meaning that the hormones are released directly into the blood, rather than through a duct), namely the pineal gland. It has the shape of a pinecone, and this particular gland is encoded in ALL the ancient symbolism.

We find it in the ancient Sumerian and Babylonian myths. Represents the third eye of the Cyclops, described by Helena Blavatsky as *"reaching its highest development proportionately with the lowest physical development."*[76] We can find it on the ancient Egyptian staff of Osiris and King Tut sculptures. We

---

[76] H. P. Blavatsky, *The Secret Doctrine, The synthesis of Science, Religion and Philosophy*, originally published in 1888, Theosophical University Press, HTML version ISBN 1-55700-124-3, Vol. 2, pg. 299 (http://www.theosociety.org/pasadena/sd/sd-hp.htm)

encounter it in the kundalini serpents in yogic traditions and, in plain sight, in Vatican's Fontana della Pigna (the gigantic statue of the pine cone). It is associated by Buddhists with a symbol of spiritual awakening. In Hindu beliefs represents the "third eye" chakra (the seat of intuition and clairvoyance), while the "father of modern Western Philosophy", René Descartes called it *"the principal seat of the soul, and the place in which all our thoughts are formed"*.[77]

If we analyse the pineal gland from Chemistry's point of view, we'll see that it is responsible for the production of melatonin, which, for our chemists' friends, has the following the chemical formula: $C_{13}H_{16}N_2O_2$ (and you can check out the mighty *'water former'* subscripts, to understand its importance).

Melatonin is a hormone that communicates information about environmental lightning to various parts of the body. And when we're talking about "light", we have to remember that we are not referring only to visible light. That's just a tiny, narrow band of electromagnetic radiation from the whole spectrum. (Google images for electromagnetic spectrum and you'll see what I mean).

Melatonin has a crucial role in regulating sleep and wakefulness in animal bodies[78] and acts as a first line defence against oxidative stress in plants[79]. It has an important role in protecting the nuclear and mitochondrial DNA (nDNA and mtDNA)[80], and is also involved in many physiological processes, such as blood pressure, oncogenesis (the process through which healthy cells become transformed into cancer cells), immune function and many others.[81]

As you can see, this natural occurring hormone has a huge influence upon our general health and well-being. Sadly, many people are unbalancing their natural melatonin production by ingesting the famous pills with the same name, available (at least in the U.S.A) with no prescription, over-the-counter, as "dietary supplements".

---

[77] René Descartes, *The Philosophical Writings of Descartes: Volume 3, The Correspondence*, Translated by John Cottingham, Dugald Murdoch, Robert Stoothoff and Anthony Kenny, Cambridge University Press, 1991, p. 143 (AT III:19)

[78] Rüdiger Hardeland, S.R. Pandi-Perumal, Daniel P. Cardinali, *Melatonin*, The International Journal of Biochemistry & Cell Biology, Vol. 38, Issue 3, March 2006, Pages 313-316, https://doi.org/10.1016/j.biocel.2005.08.020

[79] Dun-Xian Tan, Rudiger Hardeland, Lucien C. Manchester, Ahmet Korkmaz, Shuran Ma, Sergio Rosales-Corral, Russel J. Reiter; *Functional roles of melatonin in plants, and perspectives in nutritional and agricultural science*, Journal of Experimental Botany, Vol. 63, Issue 2, 1 January 2012, Pages 577–597, https://doi.org/10.1093/jxb/err256

[80] REITER, R. J., ACUÑA-CASTROVIEJO, D., TAN, D.-X. and BURKHARDT, S. (2001), *Free Radical-Mediated Molecular Damage*. Annals of the New York Academy of Sciences, 939: 200–215. doi:10.1111/j.1749-6632.2001.tb03627.x

[81] Altun, A. and Ugur-Altun, B. (2007), *Melatonin: therapeutic and clinical utilization*. International Journal of Clinical Practice, Volume 61, Issue 5, May 2007, Pages 835–845. doi:10.1111/j.1742-1241.2006.01191.x

But let's return to the flow of the electric activity between our heart and our brain. We have the heart in the chest, and above, in the skull, the brain. The electric impulses emitted by the heart are traveling up into the brain, where the connection between the right and the left hemisphere is made by the corpus callosum. Now, can you see a cross? The long arm of the cross goes from the heart to the brain, while the smaller arm connects the brain's left and right hemispheres.

The cross is another popular ancient symbol encountered in countless spiritual beliefs. Although its meaning got a little changed in some religions, in the ancient traditions the cross represented the ascension of one's soul (the long arm) when passing through a plain of existence (represented by the smaller arm).

Therefore, the more balanced we are ("listening" to both feelings and reason), the more we become "one with the Universe" (I know it's a cliché, but it's true). All we have to do is to embrace the flow that runs through our bodies, appreciate every experience, information or knowledge, and share in their turn that knowledge.

Because, here's another thing. Some might say that information is knowledge, and knowledge is power. Well, not quite, because we are "bathing" into an ocean of information. We constantly pick some information from that ocean of knowledge (for example, you, now, by reading this book). Truth is that only if we share in our turn that information, then (and only then) knowledge turns into power. Else, if we keep that information to ourselves, it becomes a secret. And when it comes about secrets, we find in the Bible (and in many other traditions around the world) that: *"There is nothing concealed that will not be disclosed, and nothing hidden that will not be made known."* (Luke 12:2, Mark 4:22, Matthew 10:26, or Luke 8:17).

Thus, returning to the amazing water and our forefathers' beliefs, we can definitely agree that the ancient books and manuscripts are not just a bunch of mumbo-jumbos. Especially regarding their records regarding water.

And… there's a little more. If we analyse closely the ancient religious teachings, every single one of them, regardless in what part of the world we'd travel (the Tanakh, the Vedas, the Bible, the Qur'an, and so on), all of them advise and encourage us to be more honest, grateful, humble, loving, compassionate, to care more about others and help each other, to be more forgiving and good one with each other.

From water's perspective, we're nothing more than little drops of water, sharing a single home, a wonderful Blue Planet, a tiny drop of chemical elements in the immense Universe.

And, our forefathers were right...

Without Love, life on this Blue Planet would not exist. Without Love and Gratitude, we can't have friends, relationships or a family. Without our parents' Love and Care we wouldn't have the ability to grow up, to learn how to take the first steps in life, to learn how to use words and create sentences, to learn from our (and others) mistakes, and to share with others the information we learned. Without Love we wouldn't have the ability to forgive other's mistakes. We might say that "Love is the answer", although sometimes turns to be "blind".

Thus, the more honest, understanding, compassionate, grateful, kind and selflessness we become, the more the water in our bodies is changing.

Through water we are links in an endless sea of energy fields, being both receivers and sources of information. Every action we make, every thought we have, every emotion or uttered word, becomes in its turn, carried by water, a source of information for our environment, for our Blue Planet, and the whole Universe.

* * * * * *

"We must begin by learning what it means to have enough... to feel gratitude for having been born on a planet so rich in nature and gratitude for the water that makes our life possible. If you open your eyes you will see that the world is full of so much that deserves our gratitude. When you have become the embodiment of gratitude, think about how pure the water that fills your body will be. When this happens, you, yourself will be a beautiful shining crystal of light."
Masaru Emoto (1943 – 2014)

* * * * * *

In the hope that you will try as much as possible to imbibe the information presented in the book, please try to reach out to your loved ones and bless them with your recently gained knowledge.

Thank You Very Much. Love and Gratitude.

Printed in Great Britain
by Amazon

36987816R00047